St. Josepn

Guide to the Bible

*Becoming Comfortable with the Bible
in Four Simple Steps*

Karl A. Schultz

CATHOLIC BOOK PUBLISHING CORP.
New Jersey

NIHIL OBSTAT: Rev. Donald E. Blumenfeld, Ph.D.
          Censor Librorum

IMPRIMATUR: ✣ Most Rev. John J. Myers, J.C.D., D.D.
          Archbishop of Newark

(T-656)

ISBN 978-0-89942-657-0

Printed in U.S.A.

www.catholicbookpublishing.com

Table of Contents

DEDICATION

To my mother and father who have supported me in my love affair with the Bible.

Acknowledgments

Thanks to Mark (Muggy Boo, Moo) and Brian for their brotherly love and support.

I am grateful to Fr. Tim for all his guidance, support, and encouragement.

"The Commodore" Neal is a good support and friend to talk to.

My appreciation and respect to Andy for all he has been and done for us.

Kudos to Emilie Cerar, my editor, for her cooperation and support.

Foreword

IT is over forty years since *The Dogmatic Constitution on Divine Revelation* was promulgated at the Second Vatican Council. This remarkable document awakened a deep interest in Sacred Scripture among Catholics. Over time many books, tapes, disks, videos, lectures, and study groups appeared and greatly stimulated a love of the Bible. Fruitful dialogue with Protestant and Orthodox communities broke down barriers. This led to pastoral enrichment in a common translation of the Bible, a common lectionary for worship, and a possible reconciliation of doctrinal differences, e.g., justification by faith alone, primacy of the Papacy, the nature of the Sacraments, to name but a few. This constitution is indeed a landmark document whose potential is yet to be realized.

That potential for the individual is what Karl Schultz's *St. Joseph Guide to the Bible* is all about. The inspired writers of the Bible did not write for scholars or those experts in language, theology or interpretation. They wrote for the average person. They wrote so that people would learn to know, love, and trust God. As that profound reality was embraced, people would "come to believe that Jesus is the Messiah, the Son of God" (John 20:31).

In a deceptively simple format, Karl Schultz invites the reader (or potential reader) of the Bible to become comfortable with the Word of God by learning how to select a Bible, how to plot out a reading plan, how to pray with and in the Sacred Scriptures, and how to make practical applications of the Bible's message to one's own life. Most exciting in this format is Chapter Three on praying the Bible. Schultz utilizes here the time-honored tradition of *lectio divina,* so praised by Popes Paul VI, John Paul II and Benedict XVI. *Lectio divina* is a method of praying the Scriptures by slowing down as one reads, assimilating, tasting God's Word. Prayer like this discerns the signs of the time, reflects on the meaning with Christian sensitivity, erupts in exclamations of praise, thanks, sorrow and pleading, and, should God so beckon, rests in contemplative gaze. This gentle, yet powerful prayer allows God to enter our lives in a profound way.

The reader of the *St. Joseph Guide to the Bible* is in store for a wonderful journey into God's covenant of love. The response is that of Peter: "Lord you know everything; you know that I love you" (John 21:17). Karl Schultz will draw you into that response joyfully, so that you cannot wait to reach for your Bible again and again.

(Rev.) Timothy Fitzgerald, C.P., S.T.D.
St. Paul Monastery, Pittsburgh, PA

Introduction

My Beginning with the Bible

WHEN I became interested in the Bible as a college freshman, I didn't look around for books on the Bible. I wanted to go directly to the source, and discover what it had to say. Much of it was familiar from my attendance at Mass, Catholic grade school, and CCD (Sunday school), but there was also much I had missed or forgotten.

I benefited enormously from getting right into the Bible. Ignorance was bliss, and I went a long way on sincerity and enthusiasm.

The experience of first encountering the Bible, like a conversion or new love, can be euphoric at first. However, it is how we respond after the honeymoon period is over, when the inevitable dryness, discouragement, and confusion set in, that determines the long-term efficacy of our endeavor.

I was blessed to have the support of a Protestant friend who was well-versed in the Bible. I had the correct instincts to stay mostly in the New Testament while dabbling periodically in familiar sections of the Old Testament. I read Paul's letters and the other epistles because I wasn't as familiar with them as I was with the Gospels. I soon found out that St. Peter was right: St. Paul can be difficult to understand (cf. 2 Pt

3:15-16). Nonetheless, he speaks to me like few others can, and I continually rediscover how worthy his writings are of my attention and energies.

After several months of reading the Bible daily, my hunger for the Word expanded. The questions and confusion that arose during my reading sessions multiplied, and I felt drawn to learn more about the Bible. Like the Ethiopian eunuch pondering the prophecies of Isaiah (cf. Acts 8:26-40), I needed help in understanding what I was reading so that I could interpret and pray with it more effectively.

Reading two classic introductions to the Bible, *Reading Scripture as the Word of God* by George Martin and *Background to the Bible* by Richard T.A. Murphy, O.P., further whetted my appetite.

The university library had a copy of the *Jerome Biblical Commentary,* which in its revised version remains the standard Catholic commentary on the Bible in English. I have discovered much about the Bible through ongoing reading. A little can go a long way when we work with God.

Because I started at a relatively young age (during adolescence would have been better, but I was preoccupied with my basketball career), I had plenty of time to get directly acquainted with the Bible, to concentrate on the Bible rather than on books on the Bible. For this I am thankful. Only after college did I get more involved in Bible study and background reading.

Finding Your Path

Each of us has our own path to the Bible and to the Lord. I can offer pointers and directions, but not a precise roadmap. I am still fine-tuning the approach that works for me, and I've written eleven books on the subject!

Life and providence are not static. As circumstances change, so must we. When we think we've arrived we can be sure that we haven't.

Why All the Fuss?

Perhaps you are wondering, why you should read a book about the Bible at all? In looking back I recognize that I would have benefited considerably from a short and sweet introduction to the Bible. This would have shown me how and where to begin, and how to proceed, while providing a foundation for further inquiry. A basic map can point out directions, markers, terrain, roadblocks, and blind alleys.

Exploring the Bible without any kind of aid has its adventurous element. It forces us to use logic and intuition, and fosters confidence in our reading and interpretive abilities. However, we are better off with basic guidance from competent authorities. Better to build on the wisdom and experience of others than to reinvent the wheel. Of course, the other extreme—relying passively on others for instruction and initiative—has its own pitfalls. To paraphrase Einstein, the process must be made as simple as possible, but not simpler.

A little preparation can go a long way. In an analogy that you will soon become familiar with, it is like the dating process. You have to be yourself and learn as you go along, but it helps to receive guidance. The Bible and life, like the opposite sex, are a mystery, and we can use all the competent counsel and direction we can get.

Grass-roots Participation

It was not only reflection on my own experience that led me to write this book. Feedback from my previous books on the Bible convinced me that I needed to offer a more basic level of instruction.

I have always tried to make my books relevant to persons at all levels of Bible familiarity. In the process, I necessarily included information of an advanced nature. This benefits the reader significantly, as it trains them to approach the Bible competently and confidently, but it also requires more time and effort. I wanted my books to be accessible, enjoyable, and manageable, but also challenging.

A wonderful thing about the Bible is that it is written for everyone. Persons learned in the Bible can communicate to novices the fundamentals necessary for a competent understanding and a fulfilling experience. With guidance, preparation, attentiveness, and perseverance, sincere readers can make significant strides in their relationship with the Bible in a relatively short time.

Few other disciplines allow novices to progress so rapidly. Morally and spiritually, we're all on equal footing with God and the Bible, and the Holy Spirit and Church are here to help us, so there is a relative-

With guidance, preparation, attentiveness, and perseverance, sincere readers can make significant strides in their relationship with the Bible in a relatively short time.

ly short indoctrination period. Of course, the learning process never ends, and the Bible never ceases to be challenging, and at times, perplexing.

I am of the opinion that overly simplified and passive education does a disservice to the learner. We can see the damage it does to society. We allow mindless and sometimes deviant entertainment and advertising to condition us, and one-dimensional and often dysfunctional personalities (e.g., athletes, entertainers, celebrities) to fascinate us.

As a former athlete (a brief basketball career at the University of Michigan), I know that no one improves without being stretched out of their comfort zone. At the same time, limits and boundaries are necessary. I will try to walk this fine line in this book. You will be the judge of the degree to which I have succeeded.

New Wine for New Wineskins

As the subtitle indicates, I have endeavored to provide you with what you need to know to begin reading, praying, and interpreting the Bible in a competent and confident manner. I have sought suggestions and feedback from numerous readers who are new to the Bible. A few were familiar with my other books so they could point out areas where the material bordered on duplication. There is no substitute for listening to those in the trenches. Many of their concerns have been addressed and their insights and comments incorporated in this book.

I began leading Bible sharing groups in 1983, almost 25 years ago. I have led them in diverse environments and encountered a variety of backgrounds and perspectives. I have had an ongoing stream of input and feedback from participants that has significantly shaped my perspective on the Bible and how to teach it to beginners. I am still learning.

The more I know the humbler I get. Being reminded of all that you don't know helps you maintain a balanced perspective. This book contains some of the riper fruits of my education and formation process. Your response and feedback will be the seed of my future efforts.

I made a conscious effort to avoid duplicating material contained in my introductions to the Bible (*The How-To Book of the Bible,* Our Sunday Visitor, 2004), and to *Lectio Divina* (*How to Pray with the Bible: The Ancient Prayer Form of Lectio Divina Made Simple,* Our Sunday Visitor, 2007). These books make excellent follow-ups and companions to this book, but they are not a replacement.

Let's Get to It!

Every book I have ever written has exceeded the intended page count—except this one. I have endeavored to make this book succinct, simple, and straightforward. I resisted every temptation to include unnecessary information. To quench any lingering thirst for information and guidance on particular subjects, I will refer you to the appropriate sources. My intention with this book is to keep you focused on the Bible.

Translation Used and Biblical Abbreviations

I reference biblical passages throughout the book not only as a basis and justification for my comments, but also to familiarize you with the Bible. As you read this book, return to the Bible at every inclination and opportunity. Whether to follow up on one of my biblical cross-references, or to continue to satisfy your spiritual thirst and curiosity, put this book down and go to the source. The following pointers will help you find your way around the Bible and discover the Bible's cohesiveness and consistency.

When quoting from the Bible, this book uses the *Revised Standard Version*, Catholic Edition, because it is both literal and accessible (i.e., comprehensible to persons without a background in the Bible). You do not need to use the same translation to follow along.

The *New American Bible* (which is used in the American liturgy and Lectionary), the *New Jerusalem Bible,* and the *New Revised Standard Version, Catholic Edition,* are other fine Catholic translations. See *The How-To Book of the Bible* for a more extensive discussion of translation characteristics and differences.

For flow and space reasons, I frequently provide biblical cross-references (i.e., citations such as Gal 2 or 1 Sam 9) rather than direct quotations. The following is the system commonly used for referencing the Bible. Abbreviations of biblical books vary slightly by translation, but are easy to decipher. They can be found in your Bible's table of contents.

Deciphering a Biblical Reference

The following are some helpful hints for understanding biblical references:

- A biblical reference begins with the abbreviation of the biblical book, e.g., Gen for Genesis. The abbreviation is not followed by a period. A number before the abbreviation indicates the first, second, or third book of that name. For example, 3 Jn refers to the third letter of John, and 2 Cor refers to the second letter of St. Paul to the Corinthians.
- The number after the biblical abbreviation is the chapter. For example, Mk 8 refers to the eighth chapter of Mark. If the reference points to a spe-

cific verse(s), it will continue with a colon, then the verse number. For example, Lk 2:4 means the fourth verse of chapter two of Luke.

- A series of verses within the same chapter are designated by a hyphen. For example, Num 4:1-7 means verses one through seven of the fourth chapter of Numbers.

  A sequence of chapters within the same book is also designated by a hyphen. Jn 13-17 refers to the thirteenth through seventeenth chapters of the Gospel of John. Remember, a colon is necessary to designate a verse.

- Commas separate discontinuous verses within the same chapter. For example, Mk 3:1, 6, 7 means the first, sixth, and seventh verses of chapter three of Mark's Gospel.

- Semicolons distinguish different chapters. For example, Eccl 3:7; 5:8, means the seventh verse of chapter three of Ecclesiastes and the eighth verse of chapter five. Dt 3; 7; 9 means the third, seventh, and ninth chapters of Deuteronomy. Remember, a colon is necessary to indicate specific verses.

  If more than one biblical book is referenced, it will be contained in a separate designation and separated by a semicolon, for example, Jn 3:3; Ps 1:2.

  Decipher this one: Mt 3:4, 6; 4:5-8; 10:1 (the Gospel of Matthew, verses four and six of chapter three, verses five through eight of chapter four, and verse one of chapter ten).

- The letters "f." or "ff." following a biblical reference mean the verse(s) designated and those that follow. Scholars use this with the assumption that their reader will know from the context how far to read.

  The term "cf." means cross-reference, and precedes a passage(s) that is referenced but not quoted. If a passage is quoted verbatim, its reference will not be preceded by a "cf."

- When a reference ends in a, b, or c, it refers to the first, second, or third part of a verse that is lengthy or reflects a break in thought. Such detail occurs mostly in scholarly writings.

—————— ✨ ——————

It is the biblical text that is inspired. The verse numbering system came more than a millennium after the final book of the Bible was written.

—————— ✨ ——————

Occasionally we encounter passages in which the chapter and verse designations do not accurately reflect breaks in the text. It is the biblical text that is inspired. The verse numbering system came more than a millennium after the final book of the Bible was written.

Gen 2:4 illustrates both of the above. "This was the origin of the heavens and the earth when it was first created. When the Lord God made the heavens and the earth, . . ." The first half of the verse, identified as Gen 2:4a, concludes the first creation story (Gen 1:1-

2:4a), and the second half of the verse, Gen 2:4b, begins the second creation story (Gen 2:4b-3:24).

I use the term "Old Testament" rather than the more ecumenical term "Hebrew Scriptures," because I am including in my reference the seven books and additional material included in the Catholic Bible but excluded from the Jewish and Protestant canon. I ask that persons who prefer the more ecumenical expression bear with my usage and make a mental substitution.

Feedback

The subtitle of this book promises guidance on becoming comfortable with the Bible in four simple steps. This assertion was not made glibly or frivolously. Each step is equivalent to one chapter or subject: Resources (Selecting a Bible), Strategy (Developing a Reading Plan), Model (How to Practice *Lectio Divina*), and Interpretation and Applications. You are the judge of the degree to which I have fulfilled this promise. I invite you to share your verdict with me and others.

Your feedback helps refine my faith and message. I welcome your insights, stories, and suggestions. Contact me at my web site (www.karlaschultz.com), e-mail me at karlaschultz@juno.com, or write to me at Genesis Personal Development Center, 3431 Gass Avenue, Pittsburgh, PA 15212-2239. The telephone number is (412) 766-7545. I look forward to hearing from you, and wish you well on your journey.

Chapter One

Selecting a Bible

SINCE our objective is to get started on the Bible right away, we'll begin with basic information on acquiring a suitable translation and Bible. We will also discuss a helpful tool for understanding the Gospels in their historical and theological context.

First Things First: Steps for Starting Out

The first thing you must do is get a Bible. If you have one already, use it until you have a chance to consider your needs and ponder the guidelines below for choosing a translation and purchasing a new Bible.

If the Bible at hand is a recent translation and you are comfortable with it, you might consider using it for the near future. The longer you read the Bible, the clearer will be your objectives and preferences in reading it.

When you decide that it is time for a new Bible, read the guidelines below, and if you would like further guidance, consult the detailed guide to translations found in chapter four of my *The How-To Book of the Bible*.

Searching for a New Bible: Where to Begin

The best place to begin your search for a new Bible is at the library or bookstore. The latter will have the latest editions. You can also do a search on the Internet, but it is easier to determine a Bible's suitability when you have it in your hands rather than as an image on the screen.

Criteria for Choosing a Bible

While the translation is probably the most important consideration when choosing a Bible, there are other important criteria to consider. These include typeface and font size, page layout, margins (some Bibles have wide margins that facilitate journaling and note-taking), and the quantity and quality of accompanying footnotes and reader aids. You'll develop preferences by surveying and comparing various Bibles. When I choose a Bible, translation is most important, followed by study aids, margins (I like plenty of "white space" for reading aesthetics and for inscribing notes), and font size.

Catholic Bibles

In most cases, readers should choose a translation designed for persons of their faith. Catholics should stick with the *New American Bible, New Jerusalem Bible,* or the Catholic editions of the *Revised Standard Version* or *New Revised Standard Version.*

If you want a Bible with simpler language, the Catholic edition of the *Today's English Version* (also called *Good News For Modern Man*) is acceptable for spiritual reading, but not for serious study.

The *New American Bible* is the version used in the liturgy in the United States. Its New Testament, revised in 1986, includes a moderate amount of inclusive language. The Revised Psalms, published in 1991, include a larger dose of inclusive language. Its use of vertical inclusive language (avoidance of the masculine pronoun with respect to God and Christ) was a cause of concern for the Vatican, and was found unsuitable for liturgical use. A modified version incorporating horizontal inclusive language has been approved (e.g., inserting "brothers and sisters" when a mixed audience is being addressed).

I respect the wishes of those who prefer inclusive language for their personal reading of the Bible. For pastoral reasons and out of Christian charity, their sensitivities ought to be respected alongside those of a different perspective. The Church has room for everyone, and diversity is acceptable when it does not threaten core teachings and practices. There are more important issues in the life of the Church than semantic disputes, so we ought to follow the biblical principle of emphasizing what unites us and respect the consciences of all (cf. 1 Cor 10:23-33).

Study Bibles

When you are starting out, you do not need a study Bible, but one can come in handy down the road or when you are confused by a passage.

If you select the *New Jerusalem Bible (NJB)*, try to get the regular edition, which contains extensive footnotes and study aids. However, the print is small.

The standard editions of the *New American Bible (NAB)* come with footnotes and background articles that are sufficient for most beginners, and are priced reasonably. The *Catholic Study Bible* contains extensive background articles and reading guides, but its footnotes are less comprehensive than those in the NJB Regular Edition. The *Catholic Bible: Personal Study Edition* (Oxford University Press) does not provide as in-depth scholarly guidance and background as the aforementioned, and its study aids are written at a more basic level. The *NAB Saint Joseph Edition* published by The Catholic Book Publishing Corporation has been around a long time and strikes a good balance between thoroughness and accessibility.

Study editions of the *Revised Standard Version (RSV)* and *New Revised Standard Version (NRSV)*, such as the *Harper Collins Study Bible* or the *Oxford Annotated Edition*, are good but, for Catholics, my preference is a study Bible containing the *New American Bible* translation. If I could only recommend one Bible, it would be the *New American Bible with the Revised New Testament*.

Older Translations

Older translations such as the *Jerusalem Bible* and the *New American Bible* without the Revised New

Testament are acceptable but eventually should be upgraded. Translations that are not from the original languages, such as the *Douay-Rheims* version, are acceptable only until you can get an up-to-date translation. The *King James Version* is an early seventeenth century translation that uses archaic phrasing and vocabulary, the meaning of which has changed significantly. Advances in textual criticism and archaeology and discoveries such as the Dead Sea Scrolls render the manuscript basis of the translation outdated and inadequate.

The most literal modern translation, the *Revised Standard Version,* includes some archaic language (i.e., thee's and thou's) but does not include inclusive language. It has been a staple of seminary and university Bible classes for four decades. The *New Revised Standard Version* is also quite literal, dispenses with the "thee's and thou's", and contains extensive inclusive language. The Catholic editions of both are quite acceptable, but I lean toward the original translation because it is more literal and the distraction of archaic language is less bothersome than that of extensive inclusive language.

Parallel Bibles

One of the American Bible Society's most popular and enduring products is the *Synopsis of the Four Gospels.* It presents parallel passages in the four Gospels in juxtaposed columns that help you compare how the evangelists, influenced by their theological perspective and pastoral/community situation, treat the same event or teachings in different ways. The *Synopsis* uses the Revised Standard Version, and has been a standard among Bible students for over twenty-five years.

The *Synopsis* is a great practical introduction to an accessible aspect of modern biblical criticism known as redaction (editorial) criticism, which considers how the theological perspective, literary style, and pastoral situation (the needs of the community to whom the evangelists were writing) influences the form and content of their message, always under the inspiration of the Holy Spirit. By comparing the evangelists' accounts, we get closer to their literal meaning, which then serves as the basis for our prayer and personal applications.

The Three Stages of the Gospel Message

In 1964, the Pontifical Biblical Commission (PBC) published a landmark document entitled *On the Historical Truth of the Gospels.* It paved the way for the Vatican II document on Scripture known as *The Dogmatic Constitution on Divine Revelation.* Since the official version of the documents of Vatican II is in Latin, they are frequently referred to by their opening words, in this case, *Dei Verbum* (The Word of God).

The most influential teaching of the PBC document was its affirmation of the contemporary scholarly assertion that the Gospels reflect three stages of development:

- Historical stage: The life and ministry of Jesus: His words and deeds and the events surrounding Him.
- Apostolic stage: The early Church's preaching and teaching about Jesus and handing on of His message, mission, and legacy.
- Evangelist stage: Drawing on historical recollections and apostolic teaching, the recording of theologically oriented (according to the perspective of the evangelist and his community) and orderly accounts (cf. Lk 1:1-4) of the life, mission, and message of Jesus.

The *Synopsis of the Four Gospels* helps us incorporate this foundational understanding of the composition of the Gospels in our daily reading without getting involved in complex scholarly theories or cumbersome background information.

Summary

When we decide to undertake an exploration of the Bible, we don't want to spend excessive time in preliminary considerations. Once you achieve a basic understanding of the fundamentals and have a suitable Bible at your disposal, begin or resume reading it. The information above will enable you to begin and proceed in a competent and confident manner, and the next chapter will tell you where to start.

Chapter Two

Developing a Reading Plan

AFTER acquiring a Bible, one of the first questions people ask is: Where do I start, and how should I proceed? Thankfully, the proper directives are simple and straightforward, and are agreed upon with some variations by most mainstream Catholic scholars and teachers of the Bible.

Liturgical Sources

The Lectionary of the Mass

First, read the selections in the three-year *Sunday and Holy Day Lectionary,* and if you are ambitious, supplement it by reading the selections in the two-year cycle used for daily Mass. The devotional book containing the lectionary readings is known as the *Sunday* or *Daily Missal* and these are available from Catholic Book Publishing Corp. (www.catholicbook publishing.com).

The Sunday readings are grouped in a three-year cycle using the letters *A, B,* and *C.* Most of the Gospel readings from year *A* are taken

> *The Sunday readings are grouped in a three-year cycle using the letters A, B, and C.*

from Matthew, *B* from Mark (with the option of using readings from John during several consecutive weeks in "Ordinary Time"), and *C* from Luke. John is prominent during Lent and Easter of all three years and is used on feast days on which passages from his Gospel are particularly appropriate.

The Old Testament readings and Psalms are chosen for their correspondence to the Gospel selection, while the readings from the New Testament letters sometimes correspond to the Gospel but almost always are presented sequentially. That is, for several weeks we read from Romans, then from Hebrews, James, etc.

Practical advantages of using the Lectionary as a guide for your reading are that you will not bite off more than you can chew, and you'll go through most of the important parts of the Bible in an orderly, cohesive, and coherent manner. The most confusing and antiquated parts of the Bible are generally excluded from the Lectionary. Consistent exposure to a comprehensive and thematically arranged array of texts gives you the Bible's big picture, which is helpful for interpreting individual passages in context.

Such reinforcement of the readings proclaimed at Mass helps you experience them as more personal and relevant. You will join millions of Catholics engaged in the same activity. Section 21 of the Vatican II document *Dei Verbum* speaks of the faithful receiving the bread of life from both the table of God's word and of Christ's body (the Eucharist). When we read the lectionary readings both before and after Mass, we open ourselves to being more receptive and responsive to the Eucharist.

The efficacy of the Lectionary as the foundation of a Bible-reading plan is confirmed by the many books, periodicals, and articles available on the subject. A commentary in book form on the Sunday readings enables you to access insights, background information, and practical applications in an orderly fashion. Some commentaries include the biblical text, while others do not. Most Catholic newspapers publish a column containing reflections on the readings. In recent years these have included cross-references to relevant sections of the Catholic Catechism, usually as a complement to biblical cross-references which highlight the Bible's diverse contexts and big picture (overall, cohesive message).

These aids are helpful but not mandatory, particularly if you are reading the footnotes and background articles that come with your Bible.

While the Lectionary is the recommended and most popular reading program, not only for beginners but also for experienced readers of the Bible, we need not limit ourselves to it. We can also read the Bible in a less structured manner as a supplement to the lectionary readings. The Bible is a gift to us, a

———————— ✿ ————————

The Bible is a gift to us, a special medium of God's communications, and we should be enthusiastic, pliable, and spontaneous in response.

———————— ✿ ————————

special medium of God's communications, and we should be enthusiastic, pliable, and spontaneous in response.

Liturgy of the Hours

Some people might prefer to acquaint themselves with the scriptures by praying the *Liturgy of the Hours,* traditionally referred to as the *Divine Office.* Like the Mass, the *Liturgy of the Hours* is "liturgeia" (Greek: "work of the people" by which "all mankind" are lifted up to God). It is the "Prayer of the Church" and at its heart are the Psalms. It also includes prayers, intercessions, and a skillfully compiled selection of readings from the writings of the Church Fathers, the Councils, and the saints.

Through the *Liturgy of the Hours,* the Church consecrates time, sanctifies herself, and worships God (cf. *General Instruction on the Liturgy of the Hours*) and fulfills St. Paul's instruction, in accord with Jesus' command, to "pray without ceasing" (1 Thes 5:17; cf. Lk 18:1). It helps us integrate sacred and secular time such that God and His word are not pushed to the periphery of our life.

Because the *Liturgy of the Hours* is complex, attempting it can be intimidating. The clergy, for whom its recitation is mandatory, become acquainted with the structure and rubrics (directions printed in red) while in the seminary. A step-by-step guide for praying the *Liturgy of the Hours, The Divine Office for*

Dodos, is available from Catholic Book Publishing Corp. For busy laypersons, praying just one of the "hours"—especially Morning or Evening Prayer, the "hinges of the day"—is a fitting, and indeed encouraged, alternative. Online resources and print publications supportive of this endeavor abound. Joining (or forming) a parish group for community recitation of Morning or Evening Prayer can also be very helpful. We all need personal and group support in our prayer life.

Many people, including myself, simply do not have the time or the patience for the *Liturgy of the Hours* and prefer to stick with the Bible readings in the Lectionary. My suggestion is that you begin with the Lectionary, and then if so inclined check out the *Liturgy of the Hours.* Its full version fills four volumes, but it is also available in two abridged one-volume versions, *Christian Prayer* and *Shorter Christian Prayer.* All are published by Catholic Book Publishing Corp. A good introduction to the *Liturgy of the Hours* is *Together in Prayer: Learning to Love the Liturgy of the Hours* by Charles E. Miller, C.M.

A Biblical Analogy

A good analogy for our relationship with the Bible is that of intimate friendship and its ultimate expression, marriage. Friendship and marriage are composed of familiar stages. We begin with acquaintance-ship, meeting someone and learning the basics about them. Presumably we don't approach acquaintances in an intense, rigid, programmed fashion, subjecting them and the encounter to the stringent requirements of our agenda. In general, the more natural and relaxed, the better. There will be plenty of time and opportunity later for intensity. There is a time for structure and discipline and a time for spontaneity and flexibility.

How does this casual, relaxed attitude apply to our approach to the Bible? First, we make it a point to become familiar with Bible basics. Since the Bible is a book, we begin with the table of contents. We discover that the Bible is a collection of many books, each with its own table of contents, and thus we recognize it as a library. This broadens our horizons, expands the scope of our exploration, and alerts us to the need for at least a basic level of study and background reading. This is where the study aids in your Bible and a basic introduction to the Bible, such as *The How-To Book of the Bible*, come in. There is no escaping the necessity of doing a little background reading, but we should not view this as a burden. Rather, it is an opportunity for learning and growth, and ultimately a deeper encounter with God and with ourselves. The Bible has a mirroring effect in that it re-

———— ᏆᎧ ————

The Bible has a mirroring effect in that it reflects our image of God and ourselves back to us in manageable doses through the inspiration of the Holy Spirit.

———— ᏆᎧ ————

flects our image of God and ourselves back to us in manageable doses through the inspiration of the Holy Spirit.

The Bible's Context

When we look at the table of contents of the Bible, we immediately discover that it is divided into two main sections, the Old and New Testaments. The Old Testament is much larger, spans approximately seventeen centuries to the New Testament's one and a quarter, and is much more diverse culturally.

During the life of Jesus and throughout the time in which the New Testament was compiled, there was one world power, Rome. Conversely, at various times during the period in which the events of the Old Testament occurred and were recorded, the Egyptians, Hittites, Assyrians, Babylonians, Persians, Greeks, and Romans exercised dominance over the Near East. The Jewish people were greatly affected by this politically and culturally, and this is reflected in the Bible.

Because the Old Testament is much older, there is more uncertainty surrounding its historical setting. Because it is more primitive anthropologically, the thought and behavioral patterns of Old Testament peoples are at times confusing and even offensive to us. These difficulties can be managed by basic background reading and a refusal to self-righteously judge the ancients by our standards.

―――――――― ⁇ ――――――――

We want to first develop the habit of reading the Bible, rather than about the Bible.

―――――――― ⁇ ――――――――

As beginners, unless we are insatiably curious or avid readers, we don't want to concern ourselves with this immediately. We want to first develop the habit of reading the Bible, rather than about the Bible. Beginning with the more straightforward New Testament is conducive to this goal.

If our purpose in reading the Bible is primarily spiritual rather than aesthetic, we want to limit our initial reading of the Old Testament to its most accessible and important parts, particularly those that bear directly on the New Testament and are directly applicable to contemporary life. This would include the books of Genesis, Exodus, and Deuteronomy, Proverbs, Sirach, Job, Wisdom and the Psalms, and passages in prophetic books such as Isaiah, Jeremiah, Ezekiel, Hosea, Amos, and Malachi. The stories of the united monarchy, 1 and 2 Samuel and 1 Kings, are also quite familiar and compelling—most of us were exposed to them as a child.

Of course, if you are an avid reader and have a particular interest in literature, history, and culture, any of the Old Testament books (with the possible exception of Leviticus, which is mostly laws and rituals) is worth a look.

In dialogue with the Spirit and perhaps a spiritual director or guide, you can develop a reading plan suited to your schedule and capacities. For most people this will involve the daily lectionary readings or the *Liturgy of the Hours.*

Continued effort will gradually yield spiritual fruit. Rather than bite off too much and give up, resolve to take in a manageable dose of the word of God on a frequent (hopefully, eventually daily) basis. If you are willing to learn about the *Liturgy of the Hours* and adapt to or customize its structure and flow to your circumstances, it will gradually become less intimidating and more manageable. *The How-To Book of the Bible* contains outlines of these books that highlight important and accessible passages.

An inquiring, adventurous, and open attitude toward the Bible will serve us well. Recalling our analogy of marriage, we know how important spontaneity and enthusiasm are in warding off boredom and disillusionment. We never arrive at a point where we know our human or divine partner, or ourselves, sufficiently. There is always more to discover and assimilate.

The Bible Balancing Act

Because the Bible is challenging and can be intimidating at first, spontaneity and unstructured reading (freely perusing and reflecting on the Bible's contents) can offset the intensity and rigor. Balance the discipline and structure of the lectionary cycle with a spontaneous, open, relaxed, free-flowing attitude toward opportunities for Bible reading. No one is served by uptight, resentful, or anxious attitudes.

The Bible is a dialogue on salvation, to use Pope Paul VI's language, and we should approach it not only as a spiritual activity, but as a forum for discussion. Paul VI's 1964 encyclical, *Ecclesiam Suam*, and his 1975 apostolic exhortation, *Evangelii Nuntiandi*, along with Cardinal Carlo Martini's pastoral letters on communication compiled in the book *Communicating Christ to the World* provide invaluable guidance in this regard.

The Bible is a gift to us, and we can show our gratitude both by disciplining ourselves to read it consistently and by receiving it with joy, trust, humility, thankfulness, and enthusiasm.

The saints and classical spiritual writers are unanimous in affirming the importance of humility in the process of reflecting on the Scriptures. Humility mitigates the negative effects of ignorance, misunderstanding, and immaturity that accompany our journey with the Bible.

Rather than worry about whether we are reading and interpreting the Bible correctly, we should instead do what we can to advance our knowledge of the Bible (e.g., through Bible study groups and classes, background reading, and consultation with a spiritual director or confessor) and entrust the results to God, without ever using the Bible as a weapon or medium for judging others.

Ultimately, what is most important is not head knowledge but heart knowledge of the Bible, and the latter is primarily Spirit-driven, with our cooperation. If we receive and try to

———— ☙ ————

Ultimately, what is most important is not head knowledge but heart knowledge of the Bible, and the latter is primarily Spirit-driven, with our cooperation.

———— ☙ ————

live the word of God humbly and responsibly, we can count on God's guidance and aid, even though we may not understand nor appreciate His ways, particularly at first.

My Introduction to the Bible

When I first began reading the Bible, I didn't follow any formal system. I simply read it as often as I could, staying mostly in the New Testament. Because I attended Sunday Mass regularly, I was familiar with the Gospels, except the Gospel of John, which appears in the Lectionary less systematically than the other three Gospels, but I was not conversant with the epistles. Therefore, I spent much of my leisure time reading the epistles and wrestling with their practical applications. Most of these letters address concrete community situations and impart practical counsel and exhortations.

The Bible and Conversion

Our (re)discovery of the Bible can occur as part of an adult conversion experience. People are surprised to discover that, within the Catholic tradition, there is an explicit recognition that the Christian needs to undergo continual conversion in order to grow in the spiritual life. This typically includes at least one and perhaps two major religious turning points in our adult life, what some refer to as conversion experiences in the sense of the New Testament term *metanoia*, which means change of heart. Two prominent spiritual guides, Thomas Merton and Cardinal Carlo Martini, their Cistercian / Benedictine and Jesuit backgrounds reflecting the diversity of the Church, have pointed this out in convincing fashion.

———— ರಾಜ ————

Born-again Christians often view their conversion experience as a once in a lifetime occurrence, whereas Catholics view conversion as an ongoing continuum.

———— ರಾಜ ————

It is easy to fall into complacency and lose the fervor with which we began our faith journey. Again, the parallels with marriage are obvious. We need to continually start over and periodically evaluate the state of our lives and appropriately renew our commitment.

Born-again Christians often view their conversion experience as a once in a lifetime occurrence, whereas Catholics view conversion as an ongoing continuum.

When a born-again Christian points to chapter three of John's Gospel in support of their born-again spirituality, know that Catholics interpret being born again with water and the Spirit as referring to baptism, which we affirm as adults through our ongoing openness to conversion. God continually and persistently takes the initiative in our lives and invites us to a deeper sharing of His life and love.

At pivotal points in our ongoing journey of conversion, we are likely to have a renewed fervor for reading the Bible and praying. It's like a honeymoon period where the desires are strong and yielding to our inclinations is a rather pleasant experience. We want to know our partner better and will do what is necessary to achieve that.

The real test of marriage and spirituality comes later, when trials, dryness, irritations, disillusionment, and confusion set in, and we are challenged to be faithful to our human or divine partner by remaining lovingly attentive and loyal, even when it seems fruitless.

The same challenge applies to Mass attendance. Many people remark that they don't get anything out of Mass. Encountering God in His word, the Eucharist, and the community should be our expectation. If that isn't enough to satisfy us, our expectations and values need revision.

Now that we have recognized the importance of reading the Old Testament selectively, let us consider how to approach the New Testament.

Beginning the New Testament

When we are new to the Bible we should concentrate on the New Testament. It is the story of the new covenant established by Christ, which supersedes but does not invalidate the covenants established with Abraham, Moses, and David in the Old Testament.

Prioritizing the Gospels

Within the New Testament, the Gospels should always hold pride of place in our reading plan. They are the first books in the New Testament for good reason. The epistles tell us little of what Jesus said and did; they are mainly commentary on the meaning and implications of Jesus' life, death, resurrection, and teachings for His disciples and the world.

The Gospels themselves and the entire Catholic tradition affirm that the way to God is through Jesus, God become man. He alone reveals the Father. This is particularly emphasized in the Gospel of John. The Gospels are the sole inspired accounts of the life and teachings of Jesus. We can never be sufficiently familiar with them.

The Gospels are the sole inspired accounts of the life and teachings of Jesus. We can never be sufficiently familiar with them.

Other accounts of Jesus' life and teachings circulated at the time that the canonical Gospels were written and disseminated, but they were not recognized as inspired and normative accounts of the community's beliefs. These are known as apocryphal, which means hidden. They often contain fanciful stories or unorthodox perspectives such as those of Gnosticism (revelation experienced as a private, privileged, and secretive affair shrouded in mystery) or a related heresy, Docetism (Jesus only appeared to have a human body and suffer on the cross; He was pure spirit, and thus could not suffer in human fashion).

Occasionally books are published in the mass market that focus on and sometimes tout in sensationalistic terms the apocryphal Gospels, e.g., the Gospels of Thomas, Peter, and more recently, Judas, but their value on a spiritual, moral, literary, and historical level is far less than the canonical Gospels.

Dei Verbum (18) asserts: "It is common knowledge that among all the Scriptures, even those of the New Testament, the Gospels have a special preeminence, and rightly so, for they are the principal witness for the life and teaching of the incarnate Word, our savior."

The next question is the order in which we should read the Gospels. Although there is no hard-and-fast rule, we can receive guidance from traditional usage and the order in which the Gospels were composed.

In the early Church, Gentile converts were first exposed to the Gospels and Acts, then the epistles, particularly those of Paul, and the Psalms. Because of its practical guidance and moral teaching, after the book of Psalms the book of Sirach was the most frequently referenced Old Testament book, hence its nickname *Ecclesiasticus* (Church book).

The following is a simultaneously traditional and contemporary/timeless sequence for encountering Jesus in the Gospels.

Moving Mark

Mark is acknowledged by most scholars to have been the first Gospel written. It is usually dated sometime in the 60s, before the destruction of the Jewish temple in Jerusalem in 70 C.E.

Mark is the most fast-paced of the Gospels. Almost every chapter has one or more occurrences of the adverb "immediately," thereby giving the impression that events unfolded and Jesus responded in rapid fashion. It makes for an intense read. High-energy persons typically find Mark stimulating. Particularly when engaged in manageable portions, Mark's message is invigorating rather than overwhelming.

Mark serves as a good introduction to the essential meaning of Jesus' life, ministry, and message. Its emphasis on the cross of Christ and the suffering that comes with following Jesus was a crucial message for converts from Judaism or pagan religions for whom such suffering would have been scandalous, as pointed out by St. Paul (who refers to Mark several times in his letters) in 1 Cor 1:18-25. The Gospel of Mark is an invaluable resource particularly for those of us who live in western societies that have lost sight of the meaning and value of suffering and who are called to respond to the challenges of a materialistic, spirituality-averse culture with the intense immediacy and purposefulness portrayed in Mark's Gospel.

The Gospel of Mark remains a good starting point for beginners and converts also because it is the shortest, most manageable Gospel in terms of length and complexity, and is mostly composed of stories rather than teachings. Stories have almost universal appeal, whereas teachings may require a more advanced level of catechesis and spiritual maturity.

Moral Matthew

The Gospel of Matthew, which was written around the same time as the Gospel of Luke (in the 80s C.E.), is a good follow-up to Mark because it shares much of the same material, particularly with respect to the story of Jesus' passion and death, and contains the teaching of Jesus that is largely missing from Mark. Matthew shows how the cross translates to daily morality.

Most likely, Matthew was placed first in the canon of the New Testament because its organized structure and abundance of teachings made it well-suited to catechesis. The word-

Most likely, Matthew was placed first in the canon of the New Testament because its organized structure and abundance of teachings made it well-suited to catechesis.

ing of some of the most well-known Christian prayers and teachings, for example, the Lord's Prayer and the Beatitudes, is taken from Matthew's Gospel, even though the material is also found in a slightly different form in Luke's Gospel.

With respect to the moral and apocalyptic consequences of Jesus' message, Matthew contains some of the most foreboding language and images in the New Testament. Jesus' rebuke of the scribes and Pharisees in chapter 23 of Matthew and the description of the end times in chapter 24 is harsher and more ominous than in parallel passages in the other Gospels. Some of this may be attributed to Matthew's Jewish background: stark imagery and threatening language is frequently found in the Old Testament, particularly the prophetic books, and in Jewish apocalyptic literature.

Apocalyptic literature purports to reveal privileged, typically previously undisclosed, information about the end of the world and the times leading up to it. Apocalypse means "lifting of the veil," and is the Greek title of the last book in the New Testament, also known as Revelation. A related theological term is eschatological, from the Greek root *"eschaton,"* which means "end times." The books of Daniel and Revelation contain a considerable amount of apocalyptic material and eschatological teaching. Most apocalyptic works are also apocryphal, that is, approximately concurrent with the canonical books but excluded from the canon.

The Parable of the Unforgiving Servant in Mt 18:21-35 is an example of the intense, highly principled, nononsense message Matthew conveys. When the servant whose large debt is forgiven is called to account for withholding mercy from his fellow servant, his punishment is severe and disconcerting; he is handed over to be tortured. When shameless obstinacy is present, divine forgiveness has its limits. This reminds us of Old Testament passages in which God sanctions violent consequences for grave and unrepentant offenders both within and external to Israel.

Matthew reminds us that divine forgiveness should not be exploited in a presumptuous fashion. Matthew alone follows the Lord's Prayer with a reminder that we are forgiven conditional on our forgiveness of others (cf. Mt 6:14-15). Matthew's intention is not to make us afraid of God, but of obstinate sinning and its dire consequences. He constantly reminds us that there are consequences, good and bad, to our actions, and that God hopes to save us from ourselves.

Conversely, Matthew also contains some of the most beautiful and

---

Matthew alone follows the Lord's Prayer with a reminder that we are forgiven conditional on our forgiveness of others (cf. Mt 6:14-15).

Matthew also contains some of the most beautiful and hope-inspiring passages in the New Testament.

hope-inspiring passages in the New Testament. (This symmetry and balance is characteristic of the Bible in general. It presents both sides of the coin so that a full presentation of the truth may be manifest.) In my opinion, pre-eminent among these is the parable of the Last Judgment or "the Sheep and the Goats" (cf. Mt 25:31-46) which immediately precedes Matthew's account of the Last Supper and the Passion. This parable is found only in Matthew.

In direct contrast to the wretched end of those who neglect Jesus in the person of their suffering neighbor is the glorious fate of those who minister to their neighbor in need, even though they do not consciously recognize Jesus' presence at the time of their compassionate outreach. Living out Jesus' command to avoid ostentatious public acts of prayer, religious observance, and charity (cf. Mt 6:1-6; 16-18), they simply follow the biblical injunction to be compassionate, merciful, and forgiving, and leave judgment to God.

Matthew's Gospel is a treasure trove of Jesus' teaching that reflects proudly and provocatively the Jewish origins of Jesus and the Church. Its moral imperatives offer an inspired rebuttal and alternative to today's pervasive permissiveness, materialism, and relativism.

Pastor Luke

Luke is a good choice to follow Matthew because it helps us maintain a balanced view of Jesus and discipleship. Whereas Matthew, following Mark's intensity and directness and reflecting his own Jewish roots, presents an austere, disciplined approach to Christian life, Luke cautions against a legalistic or moralistic over-reaction by emphasizing Jesus' mercy and pastoral sensitivity, and the primacy of reconciliation.

Most of the parables (e.g., the Prodigal Son and Good Samaritan), sayings, and details of Jesus' ministry found exclusively in Luke deal with mercy, forgiveness, and reconciliation.

——————— ✆ ———————

Most of the parables, sayings, and details of Jesus' ministry found exclusively in Luke deal with mercy, forgiveness, and reconciliation.

——————— ✆ ———————

Luke is particularly conscious of Jesus' outreach to the *anawim*, the poor of Yahweh, those believers whose spiritual lineage stretches back to the prophetic books of the Old Testament and whose only earthly recourse to the oppression and impoverishment that they experience is faith in divine mercy and justice, manifested most fully in the next life. The heavenly focal point of the Beatitudes is particularly relevant to those whose earthly prospects are dim. Remember the parable of Lazarus and the rich man (cf. Lk 16:19-31). Luke often warns about the dangers of greed and possessiveness.

Luke's concern for and message of hope to the downtrodden of society is particularly relevant today as the middle class shrinks and the gap between rich

——————— ҩ ———————

After the high energy and intensity of Mark and Matthew, and their masculine, robust approach to discipleship and spirituality, Luke's perceptiveness, psychological and spiritual insight and pastoral awareness and sensitivity is refreshing and comforting.

——————— ҩ ———————

and poor widens and an increasing number of persons from all walks of life find themselves marginalized and seemingly forsaken.

After the high energy and intensity of Mark and Matthew, and their masculine, robust approach to discipleship and spirituality, Luke's perceptiveness, psychological and spiritual insight and pastoral awareness and sensitivity is refreshing and comforting. For example, his portrayal of Peter's denials (cf. Lk 22:54-61) is more illuminating and sympathetic than in the other Gospels. Luke narrates how Peter's bewilderment manifests itself in a loss of personal, communal, and religious identity, thereby providing us with a window into Peter's state of mind and heart that enables us to see ourselves in him and recover from our failures accordingly.

Luke's practical and pastoral message of hope gives Jesus' followers of every era the courage to persevere in taking up their cross "daily" (only Luke's account inserts this qualifier) amid internal (personal weakness) and external (e.g., cultural) resistance. Luke's intuition, sensitivity, and empathy enable us to follow and bear Mark's and Matthew's message in a gentle and prudent fashion and communicate this to others.

Mystical John

John is a paradox in many ways, starting with how beginners should approach him. Despite John's theological profundity, long discourses, and redundant expressions, many sections and themes of John are straightforward and inspiring to beginners. John contains many "I am" statements that tell us basic truths about Jesus that people of all ages and levels of biblical familiarity can understand.

The Lectionary recognizes John's eclecticism and sets an example for us by putting him in a category all his own. Readings from John are not concentrated in any one of the three liturgical years, but are sprinkled throughout them, particularly during feast and holy days and the Lent and Easter seasons.

Drawing from this, I regard John as a seasoning in our Gospel diet. He adds a divine flavor to the other Gospels and complements them. His absence from our reading diet is noticeable, and he has a taste all his own.

The last Gospel to be written, John, stands on its own, but also serves as a balance and com-

Jesus' divinity is so prominent in John that it is easy to overlook the profoundly human portrayal that this Gospel offers.

plement to the other Gospels. Paradoxically, the Gospel that most emphasizes Jesus' divinity also presents His humanity in a revealing and compelling manner. Jesus' divinity is so prominent in John that it is easy to overlook the profoundly human portrayal that this Gospel offers, as captured in its oft-quoted observation that the Word (Jesus) pitched His tent among us (cf. Jn 1:14).

A Strategy for Discovering John

For starters, it seems best to sample John and read on until you become confused, overwhelmed, or ready for a different perspective. A more systematic reading of John is appropriate after you have become familiar with the other Gospels. They can serve as a balance and foundation, as they did for the community for whom John composed his Gospel. An integrated, comparative reading will help you appreciate John's uniqueness. This is one reason I recommended *The Synopsis of the Four Gospels* in chapter one.

John's profundity merits a more mature theological, spiritual, and interpretive foundation, and his long stories and discourses require patience and concentration. Yet, his Gospel retains a mysterious simplicity that makes it accessible and inspiring to the sincere believer who wishes to join the characters in the Gospel in a personal encounter with Jesus. Our reaction to these paradoxes, like theirs, will be one of simultaneous amazement, confusion, misunderstanding, and intrigue. Both John and Jesus leave us wanting more, nodding as well as shaking our heads.

The Passion and Resurrection Narratives

Within the order described above, there is another piece of guidance we can assimilate. The early Church attributed pride of place to the story of Jesus' suffering (i.e., Passion), death, and Resurrection. We know this from the disproportionate amount of coverage and commentary given to these events in both the Gospels and Patristic (Church Fathers) writings.

Thus, while the meaning of each Gospel's Passion and Resurrection narratives is best understood in the context of the whole Gospel and in comparison to the other Gospels, we can still derive great profit from reading each Gospel's Passion and Resurrection narrative as a self-contained unit. Scholars have deduced that these were probably the first parts of the Gospels to be written. The rest of the Gospels, like Jesus' ministry and life as a whole, point to the fundamental reason for His coming to earth: to save and redeem us through the ultimate gift of love, His life (cf. Jn 13:1; 15:13).

Each Gospel's description of Jesus' origins and public ministry serves as extended commentary on and introduction to its Passion and Resurrection account.

Each Gospel's description of Jesus' origins and public ministry serves as extended commentary on and introduction to its Passion and Resurrection account. Themes introduced in the early stages of the Gospel culminate and are fleshed out in the Passion.

For example, Matthew's infancy narrative introduces numerous themes that anticipate Jesus' Passion and death, such as the death of the innocent children by the decree of Herod and the recognition of Jesus by Gentiles (i.e., the Magi, and the centurion who acknowledges Jesus to be the son of God). By beginning with the infancy narratives of Matthew (1:1—2:23) and Luke (1:5-2:52), Mark's public ministry introduction (1:1-13), and John's prologue (1:1-18), we receive clues as to where the words and deeds of Jesus will lead Him and us, should we choose to follow in His footsteps.

Acts of the Apostles

The placement and time frame of the Acts of the Apostles immediately after the Gospels would seem to indicate that we should read it after the Gospels. Acts is a theological recounting of significant teachings, speeches, decisions, and events in the life of the early Church, and particularly Peter and Paul. Acts is especially appropriate as a follow-up to Luke, given that they share the same author and are essentially one story in two volumes. Acts describes the Church's beginning, inaugurated by Jesus' Resurrection and Ascension and the coming of the Holy Spirit.

Paul's Letters

As in the canon (the ordered list of books in the Bible), we next encounter Paul's letters, in order of length, beginning with his longest and those addressed to particular communities, and then continuing with those addressed to individuals. Though they are interrelated, Paul's letters stand alone enough for us to read them in whatever order we wish. We do well, however, to read the introductions and footnotes that accompany them in most Bibles, thereby enabling us to become familiar with each letter's main themes, pastoral context, and setting within Paul's ministry.

1 and 2 Corinthians are good starting points for encountering Paul, as he discusses practical issues relevant to persons of all eras: sex, love, marriage, money, charitable giving, diversity, rivalries, and death.

If we wish a more systematic approach, we can either read the letters in their canonical or chronological order (as best we can deduce), beginning with the earliest:

1 Thessalonians
Galatians
Philippians
1 and 2 Corinthians
Romans
Philemon

Colossians
Ephesians
2 Thessalonians
1 & 2 Timothy
Titus

Reading any author chronologically offers clues as to the development of his thought.

The Catholic Epistles

After reading Paul, our next stop is the other New Testament letters, often referred to (with the exception of Hebrews, which was uneasily attributed to Paul in ancient times, but whose authorship now is recognized by scholars as unknown) as the "Catholic" or "General" letters because they have a universal audience. These contain exhortations and instructions designed to guide and encourage us to act morally and persevere in the face of doubt, discouragement, oppression, and persecution. They remind us of Jesus' parting words that our citizenship is in heaven (cf. Jn 14-17; Heb 11:13-16; 13:14), and that we can expect painful opposition from the world. Hebrews, 1 Peter, and Revelation particularly emphasize this. St. Paul articulates it firmly and succinctly in Cor 15:19: "If for this life only we have hoped in Christ, we are of all men most to be pitied."

Within these letters, a good starting point is 1 John, because it resembles the Gospel of John in style, themes, and theology, though it is much more compact, and offers compelling, concrete exhortations to love fellow Christians. Most of its teachings are simple and straightforward but difficult to practice—like all authentic morality and spirituality. As enduring truths, they require ongoing reflection, assimilation, and application.

From both a theological and spirituality (how we translate our theology into practice) standpoint, 1 John is one of the most inspiring books in the Bible. The second and third letters of John are personal, situational, and brief, and do not offer much general teaching. Read them if you wish, but concentrate on the other New Testament letters.

The letter of James is a good follow-up to 1 John because the former discusses in practical, straightforward terms how to implement the spiritual values promoted in the latter. James is one of the easiest New Testament books to read because it is essentially wisdom instruction conformed to the Gospel tradition.

The Wisdom books of the Old Testament, e.g., Sirach, Proverbs, Ecclesiastes, and Job, tell us how to navigate practical situations in life in light of biblical moral principles and human reason and experience.

James' direct tone and uncompromising morality, reminiscent of the Gospel of Matthew, make it one of the most challenging biblical books to put into practice. Its moral applications and exhortations are particularly handy in our secular culture in which we are often faced with conflicting values, confusing information, enticing temptations, cultural opposition, and difficult choices.

James also acts as a corrective to misinterpretations of Paul's distinct theological doctrines (e.g., justification by faith, cf. Gal 2:16; Jas 2:14-26), which were not uncommon in the early Church (cf. 2 Pt 3:15-16). Whenever you are confused by Paul, know that you are not alone.

The Jewish flavor of James is shared by the eloquent letter to the Hebrews. Theologically profound and one of the finest literary works in the New Testament, Hebrews uses rabbinical argument and rhetorical devices that may be difficult for a beginner to follow at first but that, with study (e.g., a commentary and/or footnotes) and familiarity, become instructive and inspiring. Hebrews is rich in insights and consolation for those who patiently follow its logic. If we apply the perseverance encouraged by the author of the letter to the Hebrews to our reading of his work, we will reap the divine rewards (cf. Heb 11:6).

Moving toward the latter part of the New Testament, we come upon the two letters of Peter. The first letter may have been written by Peter; the second one, perhaps the last New Testament book to be written (ca. 100-120 C.E.), most likely is the work of one or more of his disciples. Of course, this has no bearing on its inspired status, as attribution of a work to a famous personage was quite common in the ancient Near East and in the Bible, and the early Church would not have accepted it as inspired with its attribution to Peter if it was not reflective of his teachings.

Peter's letters can be read at any point because they are primarily straightforward moral exhortations. Begin with 1 Peter, which is easier to understand than 2 Peter and contains some of the New Testament's most inspiring reflections on suffering.

The content and literary style of 1 Peter is quite refined, leading scholars to suspect that, as indicated in the letter itself (cf. 1 Pt 5:12), the fisherman of Galilee had some help in its composition. 2 Peter was written considerably later and has more of an eschatological (referring to the end of the world) tone. The brief, oft-overlooked, apocalyptic-flavored letter of Jude is a good follow-up to 2 Peter. Both have fiery, intense parts that are more easily understood and assimilated after one has read the rest of the New Testament.

The Book of Revelation

We now come to one of the more intriguing books of the Bible, and the most misunderstood. Revelation (also known as Apocalypse) is the last book in the New Testament, and it should be last on your reading list as well. While some parts are accessible to the beginner, most are highly symbolic and cryptic and require the deciphering aids available in footnotes and a commentary. With respect to Revelation, the footnotes of the *New American Bible* and the reader's edition of the *New Jerusalem Bible* are plentiful, informative, and illuminating.

Unless you are an insatiably curious fan of apocalyptic literature and want to encounter Revelation right away, survey it for acquaintance purposes *after* you have gotten through the rest of the New Testament, and then return to it after you have more experience reading the Bible.

Summary

Let us now summarize the formal and informal approaches to reading the Bible that we have surveyed. Additional approaches that are useful but are not as universally applicable as the ones mentioned above are discussed in chapter six of *The How-To Book of the Bible.*

- I began by mentioning two formal, liturgical, Church-sanctioned approaches to reading the Bible. Following the Lectionary for the Sunday and Holy Day readings is more manageable, particularly for beginners. The more ambitious can follow the daily readings as well. There are separate missals, i.e., devotional prayer books, for each.

- Many parish Bible study groups focus on the lectionary readings, and there are numerous books, Catholic newspapers, and monthly publications that offer commentaries and other reader aids devoted to the Lectionary. However, all you real-ly need to start out is your Bible. Never substitute secondary aids for the primary source.

- As a general interpretive and spiritual reading principle, always start with the Bible and refer to interpretive resources for assistance, rather than begin with the latter and let others do the work for you. With practice, the support of fellow Christians, and the guidance of the Holy Spirit, you are capable of finding the message in the Bible intended for you.

- The *Liturgy of the Hours* is a more advanced method of praying the Scriptures. The complete version is published in four volumes. The one-volume versions, *Christian Prayer*, *Shorter Christian Prayer*, and *Daytime Prayer* are also available from Catholic Book Publishing Corp.

Exercise Prudential Judgment

The Bible is not a textbook, and reading it is not an assignment. No quiz, survey, or test will be administered. Do not feel bound to follow to the letter either the formal or informal models presented above. The Holy Spirit can speak to us through as little as one biblical word, image, or verse. You may rightly feel compelled to linger with this small spiritual morsel awhile and finish the rest of the reading at another time. God and the Bible aren't going anywhere.

Reverting to our marital analogy, a couple can experience a single touch, gesture, comment, topic, or memory so poignant that it becomes their sole focus in a particular encounter. The Bible was not intended for hasty speed-reading. It is much too personal, intimate, and meaningful for that. Take your time with the Bible, and with yourself and others too, and go with what works best for you. As Mahatma Gandhi observed, there is more to life than increasing its speed.

——————— ß∾ ———————

The Bible was not intended for hasty speed-reading.

——————— ∾ß ———————

The approach I propose for an informal reading of the Bible is an optional complement or alternative to the formal models, which have the advantage of being liturgical (we pray them with Catholics throughout the world), cohesive, and thoughtfully developed. For these reasons the formal approach is generally preferable. It provides invaluable structure and continuity for beginners without being complex or overwhelming, and helps them discover early on in the reading process the breadth, diversity, cohesiveness, and consistency of the Bible.

The **informal approach** has its own coherency and structure but also requires prudential judgment. The primary advantage of the informal is its *flexibility* and *simplicity*. You can follow the outline suggested below in accordance with your capacities and preferences.

- Begin with the Gospels, perhaps even their Passion and Resurrection narratives, and then move to the epistles. Incorporate key and accessible parts of the Old Testament as you feel comfortable. Read and pray at least a line or two from the Psalms each session. The Psalms should be a staple of your reading diet, as they are the prayer book of the Bible, and touch upon most of its major themes.

- Along with the Psalms, I recommend surveying Genesis, Exodus, Job, Proverbs, and Sirach for starters. If you like historical narratives, or recall them fondly from childhood, you can choose to explore sections of the books of Samuel and Kings relating to David and Solomon. These contain some of the Bible's finest and most familiar stories.

- From there you can move to key passages of the so-called major prophets (i.e., Isaiah, Jeremiah, and Ezekiel)—these books are too long or intense for most beginners to read straight through—and then sample influential books among the minor prophets such as Amos, Hosea, and Malachi. This powerful but complex prophetic section of the Old Testament generally requires background reading in order to be comprehensible.

- If you like romantic literature, read Tobit and Song of Songs, but don't let their sensual dimension fool you. Their insights into love, life, and relationships are profound, and worthy of extensive reflection and application.

In summary, let us take a cue from one of the Bible's greatest interpreters and promoters, St. Gregory the Great, who spoke of Bible reading as a privilege, honor, and discipline rather than a chore or burden. As *Dei Verbum* (25) observes:

> The sacred synod also earnestly and especially urges all the Christian faithful, especially Religious, to learn by frequent reading of the divine Scriptures the "excellent knowledge of Jesus Christ" (Phil 3:8). "For ignorance of the Scriptures is ignorance of Christ" (St. Jerome).

> Therefore, they should gladly put themselves in touch with the sacred text itself, whether through the liturgy, rich in the divine word, or through devotional reading, or through instructions suitable for the purpose and other aids which, in our time, with approval and active support of the shepherds of the Church, are commendably spread everywhere. And let them remember that prayer should accompany the reading of Sacred Scripture, so that God and man may talk together; for "we speak to Him when we pray; we hear Him when we read the divine saying" (St. Ambrose).

Chapter Three

Reading the Bible with All You've Got

IN this chapter you will encounter not only a simple, straightforward, and natural model for getting into prayerful Bible reading *right away*, but also Western civilization's oldest and most universal, flexible, and holistic model of personal growth and spirituality. There is no model in the human potential movement remotely comparable in pedigree, style, or effects. I entitled this chapter "Reading the Bible with All You've Got" because, as you will discover, the featured process accesses your whole self and helps you fulfill your potential. Thus this chapter constitutes an enormous investment in yourself and those around you.

One of the reasons I can confidently assure you of your capacity for getting started with this process right away is that you've already experienced most, if not all, of its stages and activities in some form and degree. You've already begun the process!

Introducing *Lectio Divina*

Lectio (LEK-see-oh) *divina* (di-VEE-na) means divine, sacred, or holy reading. Because of traditional usage (Latin was the language of the early and medieval Church) and the difficulty of translating *lec-tio divina* succinctly and precisely, the Latin expression is still commonly used.

We could just as easily translate and refer to this as listening. In biblical times books were rare and expensive, and most people couldn't read. Because communal listening rather than individual reading was the most common way our Jewish and Christian ancestors encountered the Bible, it is also accurate to refer to *lectio divina* as *listening* to the Bible.

—————— ⚬✕⚬ ——————

It is also accurate to refer to lectio divina *as* listening *to the Bible.*

—————— ⚬✕⚬ ——————

The Roots of *Lectio Divina*

Like most things within Christianity, *lectio divina* has its roots in Judaism. We can trace its roots back even further, to the first civilization, the Sumerians (inhabitants of what is now Southern Iraq). The ancient Hebrews developed the principles and practices underlying *lectio divina* both when the biblical material was in its oral stage and when it was written down. The rabbis who led Judaism after the destruction of the Jerusalem temple by the Romans in 70 C.E. further refined these principles. The early Church and the monks drew upon this Jewish spiritual inheritance in developing what they would refer to as *lectio divina*.

Lectio (a commonly used abbreviation) as a specifically Christian practice began its evolution in the second century C.E. as the New Testament became more widely disseminated and acknowledged as inspired. It was refined by desert and cloistered monks and has been practiced by monks, clergy, and laypersons ever since.

The Benedictine and Cistercian (Trappist) monastic traditions have been its most prominent caretakers, and have exerted major influence in *lectio divina's* development and dissemination. *Lectio divina* is the reading model used when the monks pray the *Liturgy of the Hours* and engage in their daily reading of the Bible.

> *The Benedictine and Cistercian (Trappist) monastic traditions have been its most prominent caretakers, and have exerted major influence in* lectio divina's *development and dissemination.*

A related but simpler model of contemplative prayer preserved in the (Eastern / Greek and Russian) Orthodox tradition is known as the *Jesus Prayer,* which involves repeating some variation of the expression "Lord Jesus Christ, have mercy on me." Its seminal treatment is found in the anonymous spiritual classic *Way of a Pilgrim.*

Applications of *Lectio Divina* to Life

Lectio was applied primarily to the Bible and secondarily to the writings of the Church Fathers (for example, Augustine, Gregory the Great, Ambrose, Jerome). Today, its application to life is increasingly emphasized, both because of our advanced understanding of human development and our existential, pragmatic sense of the intimate link between the Bible and life.

The early Christians also recognized this but didn't need to state it explicitly because they had not yet experienced the body-soul dualism of Greek philosophy and the disjointed effects of secularism whereby the sacred is compartmentalized rather than experienced as an integral aspect of life. They lived the Bible in the sense of handing it on in its primitive stages and reliving its challenges and drama dynamically amid oppression and persecution, not only from Jewish and pagan authorities but from fellow Christians as well.

The Fluid Activities of *Lectio Divina*

Lectio divina consists of activities that typically unfold in stages, though not necessarily sequentially. It isn't mechanical or linear. It is an adaptable, flexible, and personal process rather than a rigid or precise method or blueprint. *Lectio divina* is a framework descriptive of the natural

———— ༀ ————

Lectio divina *is a framework descriptive of the natural way people prayerfully encounter God and His word in the Bible and life. It is fluid and personal.*

———— ༀ ————

way people prayerfully encounter God and His word in the Bible and life. It is fluid and personal.

We oscillate between its stages/activities according to our capacities, circumstances, and the movement of the Spirit. Not only does each person process the Bible and life experiences uniquely, but the process for each person changes depending on their circumstances and development.

The Multiple Progressions of *Lectio Divina*

For example, you can begin by reading and then be led by the Spirit to the silence of contemplation. You might begin by praying your feelings and then move to meditation on your current situation in light of the biblical passage you are reading or reminded of. (See the discussion of *reminiscence*, p. 89.) You can read, move immediately to prayer, and then back to reading and, eventually, meditation (reflection and repetitive recitation).

Alternatively, you might begin and stay awhile in the silence of contemplation, soaking up God's presence. When you're weary, just being with a loved one is what you need most. The key is to follow where your faculties and the prompting of the Spirit take you, while eventually integrating all the stages/activities. You thereby balance spontaneity and self-discipline, and avoid rigidity, scrupulosity (over-conscientiousness), or laxness.

An Integrated Process

Although it is artificial to distinguish precisely between the sensate/physical, mental, emotional, and spiritual dimensions, for comprehension's sake we can identify tendencies of the aforementioned to be pronounced (prominently operative) in particular stages of *lectio divina.* This accentuation does not marginalize the other dimensions. Each is integrally related to and dependent upon the others during each stage of the process:

> [R]eading without meditation is sterile, meditation without reading is liable to error, prayer without meditation is lukewarm, meditation without prayer is unfruitful, prayer when it is fervent wins contemplation, but to obtain it without prayer would be rare, even miraculous. However, there is no limit to God's power, and His merciful love surpasses all His other works. . . .
>
> (Guigo II, *The Ladder of Monks)*

The Holistic Nature of *Lectio Divina*

For example, reading is primarily a sensate activity, particularly as practiced by the ancients (see p. 84). Meditation particularly engages the conscious and subconscious faculties. Prayer involves the emotions in tandem with the spirit as experienced in contemplation, and action is praxis, the application of our faith to life. A different human dimension (mind, body, spirit) is operative in each stage.

In *lectio divina* you practice loving God with your whole heart, mind, and strength (cf. Mk 12:28-34). Using all your senses during the reading process trans-

———— ๛ ————

In lectio divina *you practice loving God with your whole heart, mind, and strength (cf. Mk 12:28-34).*

———— ๛ ————

lates to using them more consciously in daily life. The discussion below explains how your mental, physical, and spiritual faculties work together in *lectio divina* to provide a holistic experience of the Bible and life.

As with the body, mind, and spirit, the stages of *lectio divina* overlap and work together. For example, reading and meditation are essentially two aspects of the same activity—taking in and responding to a biblical passage. Prayer and contemplation are the active and receptive sides of dialogue with God. The early Church originally described this process in terms of reading and prayer. Meditation was considered part of reading, and contemplation was part of prayer.

In the quotation that concludes the preceding chapter, the Vatican II document on Scripture, *Dei Verbum*, does not mention *lectio divina* by name. It opts for the ancient terminology, reading and prayer, which implies meditation and contemplation. The fifth stage, action, was assumed. In the Middle Ages it was specifically articulated as a stage. As shown below, *lectio divina* continues to evolve with its environment. Your mission is to discover the approach to *lectio divina* that suits you.

The Components of *Lectio Divina*

Lectio divina is a dynamic process that evolves and adapts itself to the needs of its users. What began as reading and prayer, and then incorporated the terms meditation and contemplation to describe the complementary side of the reading and prayer process, and then injected action in recognition of the moral and praxis (faith in action) dimension of *lectio divina*, can be modernized in the sense of adjusted to a vastly different social and religious climate. Pope Benedict encouraged such development, innovation, and adaptation in the most enthusiastic and far-sighted endorsement of *lectio divina* by a modern pontiff:

"I would like in particular to recall and recommend the ancient tradition of **Lectio divina** . . . If it is effectively promoted, this practice will bring to the Church—I am convinced of it—a new spiritual springtime. As a strong point of biblical ministry, **Lectio divina** should therefore be increasingly encouraged, also through the use of new methods, carefully thought through and in step with the times."

(Address to the Catholic Biblical Federation International Congress on the Fortieth Anniversary of *Dei Verbum*, September 16, 2005)

"Among the many fruits of this biblical springtime I would like to mention the spread of the ancient practice of *Lectio divina* or 'spiritual reading' of Sacred Scripture. It consists of poring over a biblical text for some time, reading it and rereading it, as it were, 'ruminating' on it as the Fathers say and squeezing from it, so to speak, all its 'juice,' so that it may nourish meditation and contemplation and, like water, succeed in irrigating life itself.

"This attitude was typical of Mary Most Holy, as the icon of the Annunciation symbolically portrays: the Virgin receives the heavenly Messenger while she is intent on meditating upon the Sacred Scriptures, usually shown by a book that Mary holds in her hand, on her lap or on a lectern. This is also the image of the Church . . . : Hearing the Word of God with reverence. . . ."

(Benedict XVI, Angelus, November 6, 2005)

The Martini Model

Cardinal Carlo Martini, the retired Jesuit archbishop of Milan and renowned biblical scholar and ecumenical leader, has contributed to the promotion of *lectio divina*, not only throughout Italy and Europe but worldwide, through his many books on applications of *lectio divina* to specific biblical texts and pastoral issues.

Because Cardinal Martini's books are translated and distributed by a variety of publishers, they often receive relatively little promotion and somehow come in under the Catholic media's radar, even though Martini is very prominent within the Church internationally.

Reflecting his Jesuit background and the need for more refined pastoral and personal applications of *lectio divina* in an increasingly immoral and amoral world, Cardinal Martini added the steps of discernment and decision (using *lectio divina* to help inform our significant choices with the inspiration and guidance of the Bible and the Holy Spirit) and the experience of consolation, that is, the peace beyond understanding (cf. Phil 4:7) that helps us perceive God's presence and guidance.

These are actually not separate steps but expanded descriptions of the existing activities and how they might be understood and applied in the modern world. It seems safe to say that life is more complex than in biblical and post-biblical times, and it is necessary that our coping measures be refined.

Lectio divina fosters discernment, which is necessary for perceiving God's guidance and initiative in our life. This leads to informed decisions in response to the message we receive in *lectio* and its implications for our life. Consolation is the fruit of the Spirit that comes from our intimate dialogue with God. It is a grace, a gratuitous gift that we receive rather than earn.

An article containing the text of Cardinal Martini's 1986 address to the U.S. Bishops on *lectio divina* can be found in the appendix to my book, *Where is God When You Need Him?* Cardinal Martini's insertions are optional for those who prefer the traditional paradigm. The School of the Word model developed by Cardinal Martini is presented in the diagram below in comparison with traditional and contemporary models.

Other Contemporary Adaptations

Modern folks are not as disposed for prayer and Bible reading as our ancestors because of the fast-paced, highly secularized world in which we live. We need a wading-in, transitional period to help us become disposed to encounter God on a deep level. Accordingly, I have added the concept of retreat and the activity of relaxing as

—————— ✎ ——————

I have added the concept of retreat and the activity of relaxing as part of a contemporary adaptation of lectio divina.

—————— ✎ ——————

part of a contemporary adaptation of *lectio divina*, bearing in mind Pope Benedict's injunction to prudently utilize new methods suited to the times.

Models of Lectio Divina

Traditional	Contemporary	School of the Word
	Relax, Retreat, Renew	
Lectio (Reading / Listening)	Reading / Listening / Sensing	Reading

Meditatio (Meditation)	Repetition, Rumination, Reflection, Reminiscence	Meditation
Oratio (Prayer)	Prayer (Active Dialogue)	Prayer
Contemplatio (Contemplation)	Contemplation (Receptive Dialogue)	Contemplation
		Discernment Decision Consolation
Operatio (Action)	Action	Action

Retreat

As both a verb and a noun, the concept of "retreat" is applicable to *lectio divina*. Retreating, or taking a break from life's hectic pace to enter into a more contemplative, receptive mode, is the disposition underlying the traditional spiritual practice of getting away for a day, a weekend, or more to reflect on God's word, discern His initiative / involvement in your life, and consider your response. You might call it an expanded Sabbath, a formation vacation, or a spiritual respite.

Lectio divina bridges the secular and the sacred in the sense that we come to it as persons living in a frenzied, utilitarian, consumer society, and seek to carve out sacred space, attitudes, and actions, re-center ourselves, and regain our spiritual and moral equilibrium. *Lectio divina* is ideally suited for this endeavor because of its facilitation of intimate contact with God and His word.

Lectio divina is meant to be a daily Sabbath moment, bridged to the day through assimilation and application of the "word" you have received. *Lectio divina* is also an experience of retreating from our hustle-bustle existence, slowing down, and taking stock of life. Even a few minutes can be an oasis of calm. View *lectio divina* as a retreat rather than a burden. It is a time and opportunity to be refreshed and renewed by God's word.

We can embrace the retreat mentality on a daily basis through quiet time, *lectio divina,* and settling and disposing ourselves for our encounter with God. This is not spiritual escapism, but a rejection of the materialistic, utilitarian concept of human beings and life that has become pervasive in society. Such a retreat is an attempt to find spiritual nourishment amid the spiritual drought of modern life.

Bridging *Lectio* and Life

I specifically articulate the retreat initiative and mentality because we need to consciously and proactively bridge our secular and sacred responsibilities through a transitional period in which we purposefully set aside time for the unhurried dialogue with the Lord that is the essence of *lectio.*

With our increasingly tight schedules, stretched resources, and tapped energies, it is difficult to find time to set aside a whole day or weekend for a retreat. That doesn't take away the need for periodic retreats or justify overloaded schedules, but the reality is that these are not as accessible as before. Many retreat houses have closed, and those still operating often offer their facilities to incoming groups for "hosted" retreats. Topical retreats by prominent speakers and authorities have become increasingly rare.

Since the time of recollection experienced on a retreat is a necessity for a dynamic and healthy spiritual life, we have to take it where we can find it, and *lectio* is an excellent opportunity for such. *Lectio* is not a replacement for a retreat, but an ongoing way of bringing retreat values into our daily lives.

—— ✺ ——

Lectio is not a replacement for a retreat, but an ongoing way of bringing retreat values into our daily lives.

—— ✺ ——

The infiltration of secular values and practices incompatible with Christian spirituality has intensified. Amid this hostile environment *lectio divina* is an opportunity for an encounter with the Lord similar to that sought in a retreat environment. The Bible and the Spirit become our retreat masters, and we emerge from our brief respite refreshed, renewed, and re-equipped to persevere in the Christian life in a hostile and complex world.

Relaxing

Traditionally, relaxing has not been articulated as a stage of *lectio divina*. It came naturally to our ancestors and was presumed. Their society was not as frantic, utilitarian, and compulsively productivity-oriented as ours. Given our fast-paced lives, overloaded schedules, hyperactive culture, and societal pressures to exclude God from our activities and environments, it seems prudent to articulate "relaxing" as an explicit component of the *lectio divina* process. We have to remind ourselves of the need to relax and give ourselves the opportunity to let it happen.

Transitioning

We need a transition period from hustle-bustle to simple presence (just being with God and listening to His word). As with loved ones who have been away from each other for a while, we need time to adjust to our environment and contemplative undertaking, get reacquainted, and acclimate ourselves to each other's presence. Forget our watch and the concerns of the moment. Move from doing to being.

We need a transition period from hustle-bustle to simple presence (just being with God and listening to His word).

Unless we are upset and panicky, we don't spill our guts with a loved one as soon as we encounter them. We ease into it, waiting for the right moment. With God, such sharing is always welcome, but we often need time and space before we are ready to unload. This waiting period can give us perspective and help us to move beyond surface emotions.

We will feel better after any cathartic communication with God, but our ultimate purpose is to discern

God's call and message to us along with our deepest feelings and insights, what resides in our heart and is called forth by the Spirit. Then we can bring this to God and the Church for refinement and purification.

So, give yourself a few minutes to relax in God's presence and prepare for the divine encounter. In the vernacular, engage in some "sacred chilling," with God's blessing—a preventative to heart attacks, ulcers, and neuroses. Hang out with God as you would with a loved one. You don't always need something to do, or ponder something intensely, or work on an agenda. Being must complement doing. *Lectio divina* helps us maintain them in a healthy tension.

Transitioning has a lifestyle and developmental as well as spiritual and interpersonal dimension. For example, instead of maintaining a schedule with air-tight connection times, inject a modest cushion to allow for unanticipated delays and a more serene transition experience. Allow twenty-five minutes for a twenty minute car ride and be more present to what you are doing. Don't watch the clock the whole time. Take in the sights and sounds around you, and listen to the Spirit stirring in the silence of your heart. The peace and poise this cultivates will spill over into your next encounter or activity. Rushing saves seconds but impedes a fuller experience of the present and upcoming moment. Haste and anxiety diminish our receptivity and creativity. This is just one example of how the attitude with which we approach *lectio div-*

ina directly translates to other life activities and experiences.

Benefits of Relaxing

Relaxing has the added benefit of slowing down our mind. Sometimes we think too much and analyze ourselves into a frenzy. Prayer is not thinking. It is relating. Reading is also more than thinking. It is sensing, listening, perceiving. Relaxing helps us let go of the swirling practicalities and anxieties that cloud our mind. We leave them in God's lap and invite

———————— ✖ ————————

Relaxing has the added benefit of slowing down our mind. . . . [It] helps us let go of the swirling practicalities and anxieties that cloud our mind.

———————— ✖ ————————

Him to share our burden, while we take on His (cf. Mt 11:28-30).

Relaxing is not escapism. It is more than a cessation of activities. Following upon the retreat stage, it is an indulgence in the Sabbath moments that are our entitlement as God's children. It will not cause us to shirk our responsibilities. Quite to the contrary, it is a gearing up for them through the renewal, rejuvenation, and clarity that occurs when we get in touch with ourselves, others, and God. Incessant activity does no one any good. It is like running on a treadmill and expecting to arrive at a destination.

Relaxing helps us step back and view ourselves and our situation from a more objective and calm perspective. This enables us to see more clearly and respond more effectively. By giving ourselves time and permission to relax, we dispose ourselves to be more receptive to God and His word.

Reading / Listening / Sensing

Reading the Bible according to the practice of *lectio divina* is unlike most styles of reading you have experienced. You read slowly, reflectively, repetitively, and rhythmically. It's not speed-reading. With practice, you'll develop a rhythm that facilitates internalization of God's word.

Read aloud or in a whisper or undertone. If your energy level or circumstances dictate that you read silently, try at least mouthing or whispering the word. Ancient physicians prescribed reading as a form of exercise. When you try reading aloud, you'll understand why. It requires energy!

When you read aloud, you use all of your senses. Yes, even taste and smell. The medieval monks who practiced *lectio divina* spoke of tasting the word. In a strict physiological sense, you use your tasting capacities by mouthing or speaking the words.

Can you smell God's word? If your Bible is musty, dusty, and rusty you can! Seriously, you can try to imagine the well-worn paths on which Jesus walked, the sweet smell of the flowers, the soft scent of the breeze, and the dusty roads.

This engagement of the senses is one reason I emphasized relaxing as a necessary preparation. The more relaxed and present you are, the less impaired your senses will be, and the more fluidly and naturally you will be able to engage them.

As a holistic side effect, using all of your senses naturally engages your imagination. With greater familiarity with *lectio divina* and the Bible, your experience of the sensate dimensions of the text will deepen. When Jesus uses agricultural images, you'll breathe in the farm air scented by the aroma of animals, sweaty farmhands, and seasonal rains and droughts.

Nibbling on God's Word

In *lectio divina*, we begin by focusing on a short, manageable passage of Scripture. Precisely how much is not important. We're not concerned with covering a certain amount of the Bible in one sitting. We read until a word, verse, image, theme, or a related personal experience or verse strikes us. We continue until we feel moved to stop. We then repeat it rhythmically so that it reverberates with our breathing and becomes a part of us. Initially, don't worry about whether it feels rhythmic or not. This will come in time. As in a new relationship or endeavor, it takes time to get in synch and in a groove.

Good things come in small passages. Just as a simple gesture or brief interpersonal encounter can have significant effects, so a small portion of the Bible can go a long way. The energy and meaning of God's word is limitless.

One of the side effects of sampling a small portion of Scripture is the humility it instills. We lose any pretense of being a master of the word or of our world. In the spirit of Psalm 131, we seek God rather than personal gratification. We satisfy ourselves to be nurtured by the Lord. A small portion of Scripture, taken to heart, is more than enough to nourish and challenge us.

In devoting ourselves to a small portion of Scripture, we buck the consumer mentality of our times. Rather than unappreciatively consume God's word and perfunctorily go on to the next activity or stimulus, we savor God's word and let it permeate our being and transform our attitudes and actions. We "waste time" with the Lord and experience the freedom of the Spirit. Life is about more than productivity. Ultimately, our productivity is enhanced by time spent with God. We avoid compulsive activities and dead-end endeavors.

> *In devoting ourselves to a small portion of Scripture, we buck the consumer mentality of our times.*

What if no word stands out and we are left cold by the biblical passage? That's a great question because it will happen frequently. I cannot emphasize enough: don't focus or worry about this. Accept whatever inspiration and insight or lack thereof ensues. Efforts are our responsibility; results are God's domain!

Lectio divina isn't a results-oriented competition in which we are judged by how much we derive from the text. Whatever we receive or are denied is a function of grace, which we should be thankful for. God will provide what we need. Our job is to make time for God, offer ourselves as we are, use our resources to the best of our ability, and keep at it (cf. Mt 24:46). We cooperate by being open and disposed to God's initiative, word, and will.

Meditation

Once we have identified a portion or message of Scripture that speaks to us, the next step is to savor its inspirational and instructive richness through repetitive recitation or murmuring.

In the early Church, meditation meant murmuring or repetitive chanting/whispering. In antiquity, the most common image associated with this was a cow chewing its cud. Psalm 1:2 speaks of the righteous person as meditating on (literally, murmuring) God's law repeatedly.

The Benefits of Repetitive Recitation

Our memories are not nearly as developed as our ancestors'. We don't exercise them enough. Lacking communication storage media, they had more practice. In the early Church and in medieval times monks memorized the entire Psalter.

Repetitively reciting Scripture enlarges our capacity for God's word, just as it did our ancestors'. Not only do we remember it better, we also internalize it; it becomes part of us. Like a computer, we feed our mind and heart positive input. The better the data (God's word), software / programming *(lectio divina)*, and hardware (our attitude and behavior patterns), the better the output.

This is why we spend time searching for a personally meaningful word of instruction, correction, or encouragement. Because we identified the word or message that spoke to us, it contains energy and personal meaning. Our response to God's word and initiative motivates us to live what we are reading.

What happens when we internalize God's word? It affects both our conscious and subconscious mind, replacing our negative thoughts, images, and attitudes with inspired ones. We open our mind, memory, and emotions to God's healing touch, what spiritual writers refer to as divine therapy.

God offers us consolation and encouragement in communications beyond words. Through spiritual osmosis (the seepage of fluid through a membrane), God replaces our negative programming (attitudes, values, and behavior patterns) and data (experiences, internal images, and memories) with inspired programming *(lectio divina)* and data (God's word).

Applying the Word

The medieval contribution to the Christian concept of meditation is personal application. This arose out of analytical and practical trends in spirituality and theology that arose during the Middle Ages. We ask personal questions that involve us in the text: What bearing does the word have on our life? To what concrete actions and attitudes is it calling us?

Here St. Therese's little way is a helpful model. Typically, the Spirit inspires us to make incremental, manageable improvements in action and attitude that we can implement in daily life. I refer to them as little victories. This leads to further growth as we build on our progress and gain spiritual and psychological momentum.

When we make the word personal and practical by internalizing it through rhythmic repetition and applying it directly to our life, it takes root and transforms us, day by day, one step at a time. We accumulate little victories with the Lord.

The Role of Memory and Imagination

Because memory was integrally involved in the composition of the Bible, particularly in its evolution from oral to written tradition, it should be part of our *lectio divina* experience as well. The medieval monks who popularized *lectio divina* coined the term "reminiscence" to describe the phenomenon of one biblical text evoking recollection of another. We can expand this to include life experiences:

Our memory helps us integrate the text with our experience and the rest of the Bible.

a biblical text can remind us of a personal experience and vice-versa. Our memory helps us integrate the text with our experience and the rest of the Bible.

Your imagination can bring your senses to life and transport you to the biblical scene or project the biblical context to your circumstances. In this way you participate personally in the text, rather than as a bystander: "I had heard of you by word of mouth, but now my eye has seen you" (Job 42:5, *New American Bible*).

Prayer

We have read God's word slowly and engaged all our senses so as to make it a holistic experience in conformance with the First Commandment. We have internalized it through rhythmic repetition and reflection, and made it personal and practical through application. This naturally evokes a spiritual and emotional reaction proper to prayer or what I call active dialogue with God. In a group setting, this prayer could incorporate the needs and petitions of others.

The tone and thrust of our prayer depends upon how God is working in our life, and how we are reacting to it. We might lament, ask God for something, praise Him, give thanks, or just be with Him. Always try to include some element of praise, even if accompanied by lament and uttered through gritted teeth. If I feel bitter towards God, I can invite Him to soften my heart and heal my hurt. It is important to remind myself of my need and duty to praise God, the source and sustenance of all the good in my life (cf. Jas 1:17).

A traditional term used to describe the emotional content of prayer is the *affective* dimension: In light of my current circumstances and state of mind, how am I *affected* by this Scriptural or life passage/event? I share this with God and enter into a dialogue with Him.

Denying my feelings and experiences only represses and postpones them to another, usually less suitable, occasion and context where they may do more damage than if dealt with initially. If I don't share my emotions with God and, when appropriate, others, I subject them to being released in destructive ways and at inopportune moments. The timing of the passions is haphazard at best.

Prayer is a simultaneously natural and difficult human activity. Since it is personal, potentially intimate, and circumstantial, the less said in the way of introductory instruction, the better. Our ultimate guide is the Holy Spirit, who is there waiting to instruct us.

——— ⊗ ———

Prayer is a simultaneously natural and difficult human activity.

——— ⊗ ———

If you wish to sample the volumes of helpful guidance on prayer found in the writings of the saints and spiritual masters, begin by praying first. Then you will be in the proper mode to implement their counsel in a manner appropriate for you.

Contemplation

Prayer is the active side of the divine-human dialogue. The receptive side is contemplation. At the risk of oversimplification, *prayer* is sharing yourself and your thoughts and feelings with God, while *contemplation* is receiving Him and His communications, as best you can discern, while basking in His presence. The strenuous part of your workout completed, you cool down before God. You rest the faculties used in the *lectio divina* process.

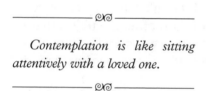

Contemplation is like sitting attentively with a loved one.

Contemplation is like sitting attentively with a loved one. After sharing words and affections, you bask in each other's presence. Words are no longer necessary. It is a communion of sorts. If this is so in human relationships, with all their imperfections and limitations, it is particularly true of our relationship with God.

A traditional and popular term for contemplation is "simple presence." The classic discussion of this is found in Brother Lawrence's *The Practice of the Presence of God.*

Receptive Listening

Another name for contemplation is *receptive* listening. (A similar term and disposition, *responsive* listening, is a communication technique.) Borrowing from the Psalms (cf. Ps 46:10), its motto is "Be still, and know that I am God." We dispose ourselves to receive God's word and initiative without conditions and stipulations.

When we are still and quiet, we are better able to hear God, and are more inclined to put our agenda aside temporarily and place ourselves at His disposal.

The Sabbath Mentality Underlying Contemplation

We have come full circle. *Lectio divina* is a fluid, circular process, rather than a linear one. We began by entering into a relaxed, retreat mode and consummate our reflections by returning there, but with the added dynamic of God's word being our inspiration and guide.

Contemplation is a Sabbath moment with a Sabbath mentality. The reflective, receptive, peaceful demeanor cultivated is designed to carry over into our activities and lifestyle. We rest and spend time with God. With enough repetition and commitment, it becomes a habit. We celebrate the gift of being God's child, with direct access to Him, albeit through a veil in this life (cf. 1 Cor 13:12).

———— ???? ————

Contemplation is a Sabbath moment with a Sabbath mentality. . . . We need Sabbath moments not only on a weekly basis but also to center and recharge ourselves each day.

———— ???? ————

We need Sabbath moments not only on a weekly basis but also to center and recharge ourselves each day. Sabbath moments give us perspective, help us center on the word we have received in *lectio divina*, and fill us with divine wisdom and peace. They refresh us, and give us energy and serenity to live the word we have received.

Contemplation is particularly difficult for people in Western cultures. Sitting still and resting with God goes against cultural preferences for activity and achievement. Because we aren't accomplishing anything, we deem it a waste of time. We are conditioned to feverish movement and rugged individualism. The idea of letting God take over for a few moments is a shock to our system. We can overcome this internal and external resistance through a commitment to quiet time and trust in God's fidelity. Even if we only sit still for a minute or two, God can work wonders in His own time and way.

——————— ✄ ———————

Within the Catholic tradition, the spiritual masters identify union with God as the goal of contemplation.

——————— ✄ ———————

Within the Catholic tradition, the spiritual masters identify union with God as the goal of contemplation. This may or may not involve a transcendent spiritual experience. Whatever experience we undergo associated with contemplation is pure grace, not something earned or merited.

It is a gift of God for which we can dispose ourselves through receptivity and obedience. We should avoid developing specific expectations along the lines of spiritual phenomena. Our actions in response to the word / message we received are the ultimate indications of the efficacy of our *lectio divina* experience.

The centering prayer movement emphasizes *lectio divina*. It recognizes that the centering prayer experience, drawn primarily from the writings of the anonymous medieval author of *The Cloud of Unknowing*, is a method of contemplation that normally must be integrated with the other components of *lectio divina* in order to constitute a balanced spiritual exercise.

Consolation

Consolation, or calming spiritual reinforcement from God, is not an actual or traditional step or activity of *lectio divina*, but a fruit of the Spirit (cf. Gal 5:22-23), a state that with grace can be induced by *lectio divina* and other spiritual exercises. It can occur at any point in the *lectio divina* process, but it most commonly occurs during the contemplation stage, when we cease activity and move into receptive mode.

Consolation is essential for maintaining our enthusiasm for reading and living the Bible.

Consolation is essential for maintaining our enthusiasm for reading and living the Bible. Without

———————— ✻ ————————

It is fitting to approach the Bible expecting divine nourishment, providing that we humbly submit to God's will, which is no easy task: "And without faith it is impossible to please God, for whoever would approach him must believe that he exists and that he rewards those who seek him" (Heb 11:6; cf. Lk 11:13).

———————— ✻ ————————

periodic encouragement or perceived progress, our enthusiasm and endurance naturally wane, whether in spiritual, interpersonal, or developmental endeavors.

It is fitting to approach the Bible expecting divine nourishment, providing that we humbly submit to God's will, which is no easy task: "And without faith it is impossible to please God, for whoever would approach him must believe that he exists and that he rewards those who seek him" (Heb 11:6; cf. Lk 11:13).

Cardinal Carlo Martini, S.J. is responsible for bringing consolation into the forefront of contemporary practice of *lectio divina.* Consolation is a constitutive element of discernment in Jesuit spirituality. Biblical references include 1 Cor 12:10, 1 Jn 4:1-6, Jas 1:12-18, 1 Thes 5:19-22; Heb 5:14, 1 Cor 2:6-16, 1 Pt 2:1-2. It helps us determine which spiritual prompts and sensations are from the good spirit (God), and which are from the evil spirit. *Weeds Among the Wheat* by Fr. Thomas Green, S.J. offers a competent and accessible treatment of discernment and spiritual guidance.

When the River Dries Up

Jeremiah 15:18 contains one of the most shocking statements in the Bible. Beset by hostility from the people and feeling abandoned by God, Jeremiah refers to God as a wadi, a desert stream that periodically and unpredictably dries up. In other words, God can't be trusted. Haven't most of us felt this way at one time or another? This is a poignant example of Scripture giving voice to universal human experience.

One of the difficulties in reading and living the Bible is that divine providence does not always supply our practical needs the way we'd like. As articulated by God in response to Jeremiah (cf. Jer 15:19), and by Jesus in the Lord's Prayer and in His response to the devil's temptation (cf. Mt 4:4), fidelity to God's word must take precedence even over the legitimate need for material and bodily sustenance. These are hard words indeed.

I need consolation when I am confused or discouraged and perceive that God is not holding up His end. The Bible consistently acknowledges the incomprehensible nature of divine providence. It always remains a mystery. God and life cannot be categorized neatly. Only through the spiritual gift of consolation is human compliance possible (even Jesus receives help from the angels; cf. Mt 4:11; Lk 22:43). Consolation is a graced (freely given by God) coping mechanism designed to help us persevere.

A common expression bears repeating: Faith, like love and hope, is more than a feeling. Consolation is not a superficial feeling of well-being and contentment. It rarely includes an extra-sensory experience of God's presence, like Moses at the burning bush (cf. Ex 3:2-4) or Elijah in the desert (cf. 1 Kings 19:11-18). Usually it is much more subtle and ordinary. Thomas Green's *When the Well Runs Dry* is helpful for dealing with the emptiness and ambiguities that are part of the spiritual life.

Consolation, a primary fruit of contemplation, is an experience of the divine peace "which surpasses all understanding" (Phil 4:7). It occurs on God's initiative in tandem with our receptivity. It is a comforting and peaceful gift of the Spirit to those who love God and do as He commands (cf. Jn 14-16). It is better experienced through *lectio divina* and other spiritual exercises than described: "Likewise the Spirit helps us in our weakness; for we do not know how to pray as we ought, but that very Spirit intercedes with sighs too deep for words" (Rom 8:26).

Action

Despite the consolations of contemplation, we can't linger passively with the Lord forever. We can't sit around and wait on God all our life; we are called to be His hands and feet, the workers in His vineyard (cf. Is 5:1-7; Mt 20:1-16). We can't let the good works and apostolic activities with which we are entrusted go undone. The message and nourishment we receive in *lectio divina* is meant to be shared.

As mentioned above, action was an implicit stage of *lectio* until the Middle Ages. Articulated explicitly by medieval theologian Richard of St. Victor, it serves as a preventative or corrective to angelism (i.e., treating human beings as if they were angels, purely spiritual beings, thereby minimizing human nature) and esoteric spirituality.

———— ☙ ————

The message and nourishment we receive in lectio divina *is meant to be shared.*

———— ☙ ————

Not surprisingly, action is by far the most difficult stage of *lectio divina*. We can train ourselves to open up to God in prayer and sit quietly in contemplation, but carrying out God's word at a significant cost to ourselves can be another matter.

So often, either immediately or soon after a particularly fruitful *lectio divina* session, I have responded to others or to God in a disrespectful way. I love God and His teachings in theory, but when they threaten my ego, comfort level, and control of circumstances, I sing a different tune. God allows these trials and challenges to humble and bring us down to earth, rather than to discourage us.

As dramatized in the Parable of the Sower and the Seed (cf. Mk 4:1-20), we encounter internal, external, and diabolical (from the devil) resistance when we receive and try to implement God's word.

Talking or thinking about the word does not threaten the world, the flesh, and the devil (cf. 1 Jn 2:16) nearly as much as living it.

Lectio divina is ongoing and organic. The Bible continually reminds us that it is not enough to hear the word. We must live it. On a positive note, action is ultimately the most exciting and beneficial stage, because it is where we bring the Bible to life, its natural domain, and experience its fruits (cf. Mk 4:20).

Action typifies the ongoing, continuous nature of *lectio divina*. Living and wrestling with God's word deepens our understanding of it, ourselves, and life. The Bible is a concrete and practical rather than abstract and philosophical book. *Lectio divina* isn't a static, formulaic process that ends with the completion of your quiet time. Rather, it is a dynamic, evolving experience of encountering and wrestling with God's word amid human resistance and limitations which, in the process, deepens our recognition of our total dependence on God. One of the greatest challenges in the Christian life is that of trusting in God and His providence amid the mysterious disappointments and tragedies we undergo as well as witness in others' lives.

The Pervasiveness of Action

More than any other stage, action epitomizes the fluid, interrelated nature of *lectio divina*. Whereas reading and meditation and prayer and contemplation are complementary dimensions of the same dynamic (holistic reading and prayer), action permeates all the stages. It makes them real by grounding and refining them in our experience. Each stage invites a tangible response (action) on our part. Action is

More than any other stage, action epitomizes the fluid, interrelated nature of lectio divina. . . . *Action is inherent in and a consummation of the previous stages of* lectio divina.

inherent in and a consummation of the previous stages of *lectio divina.*

The Integrity of Action

Lectio divina requires us to take action in a variety of ways in a spirit of integrity and sincerity. We have a choice in how we approach the Bible. For example, we can read passively and one-dimensionally or with our whole self. We can limit our prayer to a few words and then move on to something else without sitting still and giving God a chance to get a word in edgewise, or we can patiently work through the various activities of *lectio divina* in a humble and hopeful manner.

Our culture prefers mediocrity and resists those who set higher standards of behavior and achievement. Passive acceptance of mediocrity makes us easier to manipulate and control. Society will fawn over its heroes in their glory and then delight in their downfall. Individuals, families, and communities that attempt to live full, moral lives make those who do not feel envious, insecure, and even threatened. The latter are tempted to level the playing field by either taking those they envy down (e.g., through gossip, slander, false witness, or by sabotaging them) or hoping for their demise. We should not be surprised when we face obstacles in our attempt to make *lectio divina* a part of our daily lives.

We have to continually choose to give our best in *lectio divina* and persevere amid distractions, peer and cultural pressures, and dryness rather than go through the motions (what coaches refer to as "false hustle," a show for others) and settle for mediocrity.

Action is the fitting consummation of *lectio divina* because it leads us to life, the fundamental context of the Bible, where our disposition and response are revealed. Our day-to-day experience is the "refiner's fire" (cf. Ps 66:10) and proving ground of our *lectio* experience. Life is the laboratory where we learn the truth about ourselves, others, and God. It is where we bring the Bible to life, and give life to the Bible. Otherwise the word remains stagnant, abstract, and lifeless, inanimate words on a page. At its core the Bible is about life, love, and truth, because it comes from the Source of such.

Lectio Divina and Wholeness

The word "religion" comes from the Latin word *religio*, which means to rejoin. Religion is reconciliation more than ritual. A fundamental goal of *lectio divina* is to expose and reform the artificial dichotomies in our life. Maintaining these in a healthy tension helps us to live balanced and integrated lives.

The activities / stages of *lectio divina* are fluid, interrelated, and properly directed to our own and others' good under the impetus of God's will and providence. The message we receive in *lectio* is meant to be a bridge to our day, a centering point amid the various distractions and temptations that come our way.

The Dynamic, Personal Nature of *Lectio Divina*

As mentioned at the beginning of our discussion, *lectio divina* is an experience and process rather than a method or technique. We need not concern ourselves with moving through the stages linearly and methodically. In practice, *lectio* is a dance between lovers. The dance may be choreographed in theory, but the partners must find the steps that work for them. There is no hard and fast blueprint.

It's not like we move through the stages in precise order and then we're done and can go on to something else. To the contrary, *lectio* is an ongoing oscillation propelled by the influence of the Spirit and our unique capacities and choices. We can start with any of the stages and move back and forth among them several times.

Like all authentic communication, *lectio divina* is a dialogical process that cannot be programmed or predetermined. It must flow, albeit within reason-

—————— ✂ ——————

Like all authentic communication, lectio divina *is a dialogical process that cannot be programmed or predetermined.*

—————— ✂ ——————

able and intrinsic guidelines such as discussed in this chapter. Otherwise it would cease to be communication, which requires orderliness and conventions in order to be constructive and intelligible.

Our dialogue with God (often referred to as a wrestling match by spiritual writers, including some of the inspired authors of the Bible) in *lectio divina* is a unique, personal experience that transcends precise description. Its fullness is revealed only through experience and ongoing reflection and dialogue. This encounter occurs not only during our private, communal, or liturgical (celebration of any of the sacraments or praying the *Liturgy of the Hours*) *lectio divina* experiences, but as we live our life. God continues to take the initiative in human affairs just as He did in biblical times.

The period of normative revelation (Scripture) may be concluded, but its exegesis (interpretation) and application continue under the guidance of the Holy Spirit, Jesus' gift to us (cf. Jn 14-16).

Lectio on Life

Accordingly, there is no sharp dichotomy between practicing *lectio divina* on the Bible and on life. A Bible phrase may touch off recollection of a life experience which may then become the focus of your *lectio divina.*

It has always been Catholic and biblical teaching that God can reveal Himself and His word in ways other than through the Bible. He speaks to us pre-

It has always been Catholic and biblical teaching that God can reveal Himself and His word in ways other than through the Bible.

eminently through Jesus, His Son (cf. Jn 1:1-18; Heb 1:1-4), through each other (particularly those who are vulnerable and suffering; cf. Mt 25:31-46), through life experiences (cf. Ex 3), and through the sacraments, particularly the Eucharist and Reconciliation, and nature (cf. Gen 1-2; Ps 104).

Whether you start out with a life circumstance, experience, or biblical passage, applying the principles of *lectio divina* is relatively simple. You've experienced these stages or activities before; now you're encountering traditional names and principles associated with them, but the essential activities remain the same.

Lectio on Life Examples

Imagine that you are having difficulty in a relationship. Your first step is to relax and enter into God's presence. Then, use your senses to recall the relevant aspect(s) of that relationship and go over it in your mind (meditation).

Pray about it, sharing your feelings and concerns with God, then rest in His presence and listen for His response in the quiet of your heart. Elijah discovered the Lord not in the natural phenomena so prominent in pagan cosmologies of the time, but in the still small voice (cf. 1 Kings 19:11-13). Implement the message or application you discerned, the response to which you feel called, as part of the consummating stage, action.

If you are doing *lectio divina* on a circumstance such as the birth of a child, a joyful or unhappy memory, or an aspect of nature (a waterfall or stream), use your imagination and senses to bring that entity into your present consciousness. This constitutes the reading/listening/sensing stage of *lectio divina.*

You meditate by repeating (gently and freely rather than compulsively) the words, emotions, or images most essentially associated with that experience or circumstance, and reflect on how you feel the Spirit is inviting you to respond. You then share your feelings and needs with God as part of the prayer or active dialogue stage.

After getting everything out of your system you sit quietly with God, and open yourself to His healing presence and wisdom (the contemplation stage and the consolation dimension). When you are calm and inspired, you are in a better state to decide and act prudently and lovingly.

Usually you'll oscillate between the various activities before coming to a point where you feel prepared to try to live your Spirit-inspired and Bible-informed insights and decisions. This is a human as well as divine process, and thus you can't expect perfection, certainty, and ease. We walk by faith rather than by sight (cf. 2 Cor 5:7). However, you can expect growth and healing on God's timetable, and the peace of knowing you have responded to God's initiative with faith, hope, and love. Consult Pope Benedict XVI's encyclicals on these virtues for inspiration and guidance.

You can expect growth and healing on God's timetable, and the peace of knowing you have responded to God's initiative with faith, hope, and love.

Summary

We have reviewed in depth the various principles, activities, dimensions, and applications of *lectio divina*, the Church's time-proven model for prayerfully reading Scripture as an entrée into dialogue with its divine author. We have established a sturdy foundation for the development of a biblically-based spirituality and lifestyle. *Lectio divina's* many facets and nuances merit ongoing study and reflection, and thus you may wish to reread this chapter and return to it periodically.

Additional applications of *lectio divina* to topics such as suffering, care-giving, potential fulfillment, journaling, infertility, interpersonal communications and relationships, theology of the body (Pope John

Paul II's teachings on sex, love, and marriage), the teachings of Pope Paul VI, and time and stress management are treated in-depth in my other books listed in the bibliography. It is impossible to exhaust *lectio divina's* spiritual riches and therapeutic, transformational, and developmental possibilities.

Of course, it is not enough to read about and understand *lectio divina* on a conceptual basis. It must be experienced, internalized, and shared. As Jesus reminds us at the conclusion of the Sermon on the Mount (cf. Mt 7:15-29), it is not how much we know or talk about the word of God, but how much we practice it that determines our salvation.

Lectio divina can only be truly comprehended when through faithful practice it becomes a holy habit, an established and indispensable part of our daily routine. Only then does it reveal its abundant applications and innate relevance to all aspects of our life.

Lectio divina gradually exposes and removes the false dichotomy that our compartmentalized world and divided nature set up between prayer / spirituality and action (moral fidelity and apostolic outreach). These barriers keep us from being whole persons and a united community. *Lectio's* primary subject, the word of God, cannot be confined (cf. 2 Tim 2:9), any more than divine providence can be conformed to our narrow agendas. The word of God speeds on (2 Thes 3:1), and so must we in our spiritual and apostolic journey.

The Old and New Testament frequently use marital symbolism to describe our relationship with God. *Lectio divina* is like marriage in that one of its primary objectives is intimacy, and one of its fundamental modes is wrestling or struggling. As you consistently practice *lectio divina*, you will know God, yourself, others, and life better. You will become more disposed to a fuller appreciation of life, your vocation, and God's will. It will not bring you bliss, material prosperity, or freedom from anxiety in this life, but it will give you the peace beyond understanding that Paul speaks of in Phil 4:7. Peace is Jesus' and the Spirit's gift to us, and *lectio divina* helps dispose us to receive that peace, and share it.

Essentially, *lectio divina* is a model of spiritual communication and transformation. To borrow the expression used by Pope Paul VI in his first encyclical, *Ecclesiam Suam* ("Paths of the Church," August 6, 1964), it is an ongoing dialogue of salvation. Like any communication process it requires practice, goodwill, and patience.

As stimulating and enriching as *lectio divina* is aesthetically and conceptually, this pales compared to the grace of experiencing it faithfully with our whole selves, both individually and in union with others (e.g., through Bible-sharing groups, praying the Liturgy of the Hours or the lectionary readings, and participation in the Mass). It is important to bear in mind our solidarity with fellow Christians in encountering the Bible as a community of faith. As Pope Benedict XVI so often warns, we cannot privatize our religion. The vertical and horizontal dimensions (love of God, self, and neighbor) are intrinsically connected.

So open up your Bible or Missal and begin putting *lectio divina's* principles and practices into action, not in a rigid, mechanical, or scrupulous manner, but through a fluid and natural opening of yourself to God and His word and Church.

In the next chapter, we will explore important principles and practices developed within the Church for interpreting the Bible competently. This will help us maintain biblical study, spirituality, ministry (sharing and teaching it to others), and praxis (faith in action) in a healthy and complementary tension.

Chapter Four

Interpreting the Bible with Competence and Confidence

AS a reward for your perseverance on this challenging subject, we will conclude with the most tangibly satisfying and empowering material in this book: key pointers for interpreting, assimilating (internalizing and integrating the Biblical message with your whole self), and applying the Bible to your life. Continuing this book's practice of supporting your spiritual, developmental, and personal fulfillment, I will share trade secrets and practical wisdom culled from over 30 years of interacting with the Bible and fellow Christians at all levels of biblical familiarity.

You've made it this far, so I know you're up to it. Paradoxically, it's going to get more interesting and rewarding at the same time that it becomes more difficult. Grace enables us to measure up to the challenge of fulfilling our individual and communal potential.

Since we are on the verge of completing the spiritual exercise of reading this book, a cool down seems appropriate. Accordingly, I have injected periodic humor,

---- ✆ ----

Grace enables us to measure up to the challenge of fulfilling our individual and communal potential.

---- ✆ ----

broken down the text into manageable portions, and avoided unnecessary jargon and technicalities.

Rather than go into complex explanations appropriate for advanced readers of the Bible, I will provide basic guidelines that will help you interpret the Bible confidently and competently. Hopefully this will diminish any concerns about experiencing grievous misunderstandings or misguided applications. The error of private interpretation associated with Protestantism occurs only when the believer disregards the teaching of the Church and sets themselves up as the final authority on the interpretation of Scripture. The New Testament continually reminds us that if we listen to God's word, humbly and respectfully, the Spirit will lead us to interpretations meant for us and in harmony with Church teaching. Trust and work with the Spirit and the Church and there is no cause for worry. Whatever difficulties you encounter can be overcome in God's time and way.

Consider how different the Catholic / spiritual approach is from the secular / materialistic approach to personal development. Society seeks instant gratification and easy answers, whereas the Church, the community of believers, follow Jesus in seeking God's will, accepting the cross, and living life in all its fullness (cf. Jn 10:10). Paul VI elaborates on the latter in his 1967 encyclical *Populorum Progressio* (On the Development of Peoples).

The Church's Liberating Approach

The magisterium, the teaching office of the Church, does not claim an infallible understanding of Scripture except in extraordinary circumstances, such as the clarification of an important doctrine or discipline in the context of confusion (widespread misunderstandings), heresy, or significant developments in the Church or surrounding culture(s).

During its entire history, the Church has precisely defined the literal meaning of a biblical passage less than thirty times. It exercises great care and restraint both in its interpretations (the Bible's literal meaning, what it meant to the author and his community) and its applications (the Bible's applied meaning, what it means for us, and how we are to respond).

During its entire history, the Church has precisely defined the literal meaning of a biblical passage less than thirty times.

The flip side of this is that the Church grants considerable freedom to the faithful in their local (i.e., personal and pastoral) interpretations and applications of Scripture, providing that they do not contradict Church teaching or create scandal.

Thus, in either a private or group context, we can read the Bible free of anxiety over human error and ignorance, providing that we are humble and do not develop our own doctrines independent of the Church and impose it upon others. Discernment will come as part of the long range process and in ongoing dialogue with fellow Christians.

Our Partnership with God and Fellow Christians

In his letter to the Corinthians, a fragmented community in a pagan seaport, St. Paul warns about contentiousness (being argumentative); it has no place in the Church (cf. 1 Cor 11:19). In his first encyclical, *Ecclesiam Suam* ("Paths of the Church"), which was a charter for the final session of Vatican II and its subsequent implementation, Pope Paul VI observed that it is important to stress and focus on what we have in common without glossing over differences.

Advancing our own ideology or agenda while harming others either directly or indirectly is contrary to the purposes of *lectio divina*, which is designed for individual and communal fulfillment in accordance with God's will.

God relates to us as both individuals and a community. The creative dynamism of our personal relationship with God, much of which is private, is linked to our human relationships. We must be respectful of others' needs and dignity and not cause them to fall because of things we do or say. Such sensitivity is an age-old concern of the Church. St. Paul provided a convincing rationale for this to the Corinthian community referenced above (cf. 1 Cor 8-9).

As human beings we are susceptible to sin, error, and weakness in every aspect of our lives, including spirituality. However, God is concerned primarily with the sincerity of our efforts. Given good intentions, He can work with our imperfect efforts, methods, and reasoning, and consummate the results according to His wisdom and plan. He will not revoke or suspend human freedom and make us immune to natural consequences. How the miraculous occurs is a mystery.

Jesus was not spared the vicissitudes and deprivations of life, as the first temptation in the desert reveals (cf. Mt 4:1-4). He chose to accept the limitations of human existence and to live by the word of God and divine providence, rather than use His power to transcend the human condition.

If we come to God's word with our whole self, using all our resources to discern and live its meaning and call, we can trust that God will do the rest. Conversely, if we are lackluster or insincere, we will bear the consequences. Ultimately, in the next life if not totally in this one, we reap what we sow (cf. 1 Cor 9:11; 2 Cor 9:6).

Trusting in divine inspiration, guidance and providence, I offer the following guidelines for interpreting the Bible in a prudent and efficacious manner, in harmony with the Church and the Holy Spirit.

Interpreting Like a Pro: Guidelines for Understanding the Bible's Historical and Contemporary Meanings

- Focus on the Bible's message for you, and avoid the trap of applying it to someone else before you try it on for size.

"Judge not, that you be not judged. For with the judgment you pronounce you will be judged, and the measure you give will be the measure you get. Why do you see the speck that is in your brother's eye, but do not notice the log that is in your own eye? Or how can you say to your brother, 'Let me take the speck out of your eye,' when there is the log in your own eye? You hypocrite, first take the log out of your own eye, and then you will see clearly to take the speck out of your brother's eye" (Mt 7:1-5).

- Never approach the Bible with rigid expectations of predetermined results. As in intimate interactions, you are inviting failed expectations, disappointment, and conflict.

Try to seek God's agenda rather than your own. Results are God's province. In human endeavors, results are largely dependent on external circumstances (uncontrollable factors). Being prepared, sincere, and competent does not ensure results. Circumstances and other persons have to cooperate.

Bearing in mind that God, unlike human beings, always respects sincere efforts, we should relax in our approach to the Bible and accept what ensues as providential, provided that we are doing our part by using our capabilities, resources, and opportunities as best we can.

Our focus should be on approaching the Bible sincerely and responsibly (i.e., utilizing our talents fully, cf. Mt 25:14-30) and leave the rest to God. This has the effect of making us more relaxed, receptive, and responsive to whatever He has in store for us.

Such "Self-Abandonment to Divine Providence" was a main theme of the eighteenth century Jesuit spiritual director, Jean Pierre de Caussade. His memorable teachings were recorded by sisters whom he directed and taught, and these were handed down for posterity in the classic text named after his central theme. It is recommended reading for Christians at all levels of familiarity with the Bible.

Our fluidity with God's will, however we *feel* about it (as with Jeremiah and Job, we don't have to like it), complements the fluidity of *lectio divina* to make our interactions with the Bible a mysterious synthesis of human and divine influences.

Of course, this is easier said than done, particularly during dry and down times when things are not going our way. The lives of biblical characters and teachings found in both Testaments reveal that there is plenty of precedent for this. We can use these texts as source material for discerning God's will and experiencing His wisdom, power, consolation, and mercy during such times.

Remember the Parable of the Sower (cf. Mk 4:1-20). Our role and challenge is to be good soil. Reflection on the parable reminds us of the internal and external obstacles to such.

Our best is good enough for God, and it should be good enough for us. Likewise we should accept the sincere efforts of others, both with respect to the Bible and in life—especially in our relations with loved ones, where charity often proves most difficult.

The challenge is to make peace with and respond prudently and graciously to God's mysterious and sometimes incomprehensible providence, which invariably includes a healthy dose of correction and discipline (cf. 1 Cor 2:5-7; Heb 12:5-11).

- Always interpret each passage of the Bible in its specific literary and historical context (e.g., surrounding passages, the biblical book that it is in, its cultural and pastoral setting) and overall context (the Bible as a whole and Church teaching). If our interpretation or application contradicts reason or the message of the rest of the Bible, we can be certain that we are mistaken.

Biblical footnotes, commentaries, and cross-references can help us interpret and apply passages contextually. Cross-references (related passages in the Bible) help us follow the timeless interpretive principle, that "the Bible interprets itself." Of course, in one sense this is an oversimplification, as the interpretation of written texts is always dependent on the reader.

———————— ✑ ————————

Biblical footnotes, commentaries, and cross-references can help you interpret and apply passages contextually.

———————— ✑ ————————

- A key to interpretation is to keep the objective (literal, historical considerations) and subjective (personal, contemporary applications) dimensions in a healthy tension. This balanced approach helps us avoid the trap of imposing our bias and worldview on the Bible rather than taking the text on its own terms and making appropriate adaptations and inferences in order to discern its relevance and message.

One reason I provide plenty of biblical cross-references in this book is that I want to get you accustomed to looking up texts in the Bible and expanding your biblical horizons. You learn about the Bible most effectively by reading it directly in conjunction with a judicious dose of background material. Background materials should always remain a reading supplement and support, rather than an alternative, particularly when we are new to the Bible.

———— ✑ ————

Background materials should always remain a reading supplement and support, rather than an alternative, particularly when we are new to the Bible.

———— ✑ ————

To use the marital or interpersonal analogy, while you are dating, or getting to know someone, be it a romantic interest or God (through the Bible), you should spend your time and energies with the person, rather than learn about them through secondary sources and third parties. There is no substitute for a direct encounter.

- Interpreting and applying the Bible contextually includes the Church's ongoing reflection on the Scriptures. At a later stage of your familiarity with the Bible, you will want to incorporate the passage's interpretive history within the Church, bearing in mind the principle of development of revelation (God reveals Himself on His timetable in accordance with our capacity to receive it).

This diachronic (across time) dimension should enrich and flesh out our contemporary interpretations and applications and provide "safe harbor" boundaries, theologically and morally speaking, for our reflections. Otherwise we would be susceptible to fads, personal whims, mistaken inferences, and subjective deductions and lose the objective dimensions that are safeguarded by history, communal discernment, and a long-term perspective.

By reading background material that incorporates Patristic commentaries and ecclesiastical pronouncements, you will discover how a passage has been interpreted historically by the magisterium, Doctors of the Church, the saints, esteemed scholars, and the faithful.

Obviously you can't do extensive background reading and preparation for every passage, but when you are perplexed or intrigued by a particular text, it is helpful to have access to resources that will offer traditional, scholarly, and magisterial interpretations of the passage. Such impressions will not be uniform, just as the Bible offers diverse, but compatible, perspectives. If you sample not only the teachings of the Church Fathers but any period in Church history, you will discover the wide range of perspectives that fit under the umbrella of orthodox teachings.

- God speaks to His people in many ways, and we all have our own ways of communicating and understanding. The key is to stay within the broad boundaries of Church doctrine, and to be humble and respectful in our interactions with the Bible and others, particularly when sensitive human and spiritual issues are involved. Docility to the Spirit counts for a great deal, since the Spirit inspired the Scriptures and can shed light on them for us. The Spirit enlightens the Bible's readers just as it enlightened the biblical authors and their community.

The Dynamic Nature of Biblical and Church Doctrine

- Just as there is a development of revelation within the Bible, so this development continues through the evolving interpretations and applications of believers. The Church articulated its recognition of the dynamic and organic way in which theological doctrines and Church disciplines are understood and expressed in the 1973 document *Mysterium Ecclesiae,* promulgated by the Sacred Congregation for the Doctrine of the

Faith. Analogously, as individuals we develop greater insights into the Bible and our life as we gain experience and mature.

We want to avoid a fundamentalist (rigidly and judgmentally literal) attitude towards both the Bible and Church teaching. In order that teachings be comprehesible and pertinent, pastoral considerations have always been factors in the formulation and application of doctrine (and should not be marginalized by fundamentalist ideology, which is inevitably more faithful to its own agenda than the source it claims to interpret and the people it claims to serve).

- Humility is essential for understanding the Bible properly. Jesus' message was welcomed mostly by common folk (Peter, Andrew, James, and John were fishermen), social outcasts (tax collectors and sinners, that is, those who did not know or fulfill the law), and those to whom the Old Testament refers as the *anawim*, the poor of Yahweh who trust in Him amid their humble circumstances. Pride and complacency are to be avoided. When we think we've arrived, look out: "Therefore let any one who thinks that he stands take heed lest he fall" (1 Cor 10:12).

- Give little credence to salacious comments on the Bible and the Church in the secular media and in mass-market literature. While there may be snippets of truth present, their message is typically oversimplified, distorted, exaggerated, and compromised by their agenda. They have a dislike for orthodoxy and religious structures and are enemies of unity. The counter-cultural values of the Bible and the Church often evoke friction and antagonism from secular institutions and non-believers.

- In a similar vein, don't be disconcerted by biblical statements from so-called experts that seem contrary to reason or Christian values. Remember the concept of development of revelation (God exposes human beings to truth according to their capacity and willingness to receive it, which on an individual and collective level can be a long process) and contextual interpretation.
- Particularly when confronted with difficult passages that on the surface seem to contradict biblical and Catholic values, consider the biblical book's historical context as well as its author's theological perspective and pastoral objectives. Consultation of commentaries and magisterial pronouncements is helpful for gaining a broader and informed perspective.

For example, when the Bible uses exceedingly harsh expressions, it is usually because the people have gone astray and tuned out gentler ways of correction. Further, such passionate communications are a way of life in the Near East, where temperaments and the diversity of peoples, interests, and problems make for explosive interactions and circumstances. Certain people think that to be heard or taken seriously they have to resort to dramatic or inflammatory words and actions. It is obvious that this perception continues today, at a cost of accelerating misunderstandings, divisions, and violence.

Recognizing their responsibility to the Church and public as well as to God and their conscience, credible scholars and theologians avoid over-simplifications and potentially misleading statements and are careful to nuance their public comments on complex issues. They are prudent and sensitive to their audience and topic. Their deep knowledge has humbled them and made them aware of how much they don't know and haven't been able to assimilate. Accordingly, they are loath to overstate their case and engage in sensational statements for effect. Responsible scholars and theologians present biblical and Church teaching in a respectful, competent, and intelligible manner, and then get out of the way and let the magisterium and the faithful wrestle with it and adapt it to their circumstances and responsibilities.

- Resolve to read the Bible more than books about the Bible. Like Job, engage in direct contact with God's word rather than settle for third-party testimony (cf. Job 42:5).
- Don't implicitly ascribe inspired or infallible status to footnotes, commentaries, and other background materials. Sometimes they are cryptic, potentially misleading, and even mistaken—mine being a

notable exception, of course. Give them credence and respect but not immunity from scrutiny. Recognize their utility, scope (including their acknowledged or demonstrated limitations), and purpose, and both the contemporary (e.g., social or ideological trends or controversies) and doctrinal-pastoral (the biblical passage or theological concept at issue) context of their comments.

- Avoid the trap of reading commentaries on the Bible in lieu of the Bible itself. Always start with the Bible and then resort to a commentary for clarification. You'll never become competent in interpreting the Bible if you always let someone else do it for you.

As a beginner, you may find yourself confused by many passages and referring frequently to footnotes, a commentary, or other background resources. However, such will gradually diminish as you grow in familiarity with the Bible and become comfortable praying with it according to the *lectio divina* model.

- Trust the Holy Spirit and your own intuition and interpretive powers. In over twenty-five years of participating in Bible study groups, I am continually amazed at how newcomers to the Bible come up with insightful, germane interpretations and personal applications of the Bible in a communal context when they are given the opportunity to reflect and share. Reverential silence, the presence of Jesus in the community (cf. Mt 18:20) and peer pressure to concentrate foster a desire and capacity to communicate coherently and typically result in illuminating discussions.

- Having just told you not to rely excessively on books about the Bible, I am going to provide a caveat and qualifier. The Bible itself, though conducive to many legitimate generalizations and guidelines, also incorporates exceptions and deviations from the norm. This is a paradox, but the Bible itself is paradoxical. At times on the surface it seems to contradict itself. However, this is simply an invitation to dig deeper into the Bible, life, and ourselves.

The Bible, like intimate relationships (here's that marriage metaphor again!), is intolerant of superficiality. Intimacy, authenticity, and human development require depth and substance. We are capable of so much more than mediocrity, and the Bible, God, and the Church can facilitate our fulfillment.

———————— ✺ ————————

The Bible, like intimate relationships (here's that marriage metaphor again!), is intolerant of superficiality.

———————— ✺ ————————

God, human nature, and life are not so easily categorized. The Bible itself recognizes these exceptions and ambiguities by being nuanced and open-ended when necessary. It poses more questions than answers. In the service of truth, it can be coherently inconsistent, for life itself is a mystery that is reducible to abstractions and linear projections.

In both temporal and spiritual matters, the uniqueness and subjectivity of persons and circumstances make sweeping generalizations and stereotypes as problematic as rigid, unqualified definitions. The Bible utilizes both nuanced and absolute statements. It is interested in truth and reality rather than conformity and convenience (tidy theories and dictums). We would do well to emulate the Bible's discerning approach.

Martini's Methods

The biblical spirituality books by Cardinal Carlo Maria Martini, S.J. are unparalleled contemporary expositions of the nuances and implications of biblical teachings. His writings are appropriate for persons at all levels of familiarity with the Bible. He teaches us how to humanize the Bible, read between the lines, make reasonable inferences, and bring the biblical characters and events to life, both in terms of dramatic effect and personal applications.

> *In both temporal and spiritual matters, the uniqueness and subjectivity of persons and circumstances make sweeping generalizations and stereotypes as problematic as rigid, unqualified definitions.*

Using common sense, reason, and intuition informed by an understanding of human nature and the biblical context, Martini demonstrates how to relate to the Bible—its characters, events, teachings, challenges, and authors (especially the main one, God). His dialogical, imaginative, and contemplative approach avoids hyper-critical literalism (rigid adherence to surface meanings and obsession with technicalities), fundamentalism (over-simplifications), and moralism (being judgmental).

My reading of Martini's books over the past two decades has yielded an osmotic effect: his approach has rubbed off on me; I find myself emulating his methods and logic and consequently feel more empowered and enthusiastic with regard to both the Bible and life. The Bible is God's gift to us, a privileged forum of communication, and we should approach it joyfully and expectantly rather than with trepidation.

Besides being the emeritus archbishop of Milan and a Church and ecumenical leader, Cardinal Martini is an internationally-renowned text critic, meaning that he is an expert in the biblical (and cognate, i.e., related) languages and manuscripts. Textual criticism involves determining the most accurate composite text from which to translate.

Remember that everything was done manually in biblical times and during the early centuries of the Christian era. Data storage was at a primitive stage. The raw materials, instruments, and tools were awkward, the work tedious, and the scribes were sometimes overzealous in making what they perceived as corrections, thereby making the process more susceptible to error. Amazingly, most variances (discrepancies) among the manuscripts are minor and easily explained (e.g., transposition, misspelling), and the basic principles of this advanced science (textual criticism) are accessible to the average person.

Cardinal Martini's knowledge of the original languages enables him to bring out nuances in passages that less proficient scholars and teachers might miss. This is invaluable in arriving at the human element in the Scriptures that helps us relate to them.

For example, in his book *Women in the Gospels*, in discussing the story of Martha and Mary in Lk 10:38-42, Martini points out that, whereas most translations describe Martha as anxious or distracted with much serving, the Greek text implies a physical straining or spasmodic reaction.

I suspect that most of us have some recollection of a woman obsessed with domesticity and hospitality frantically preparing a large meal without sufficient help and beginning to have a disjointed physical and emotional reaction. The Gospel unfolds before our very eyes and in direct correspondence to our experience. Martini's accessible and judicious exposition of the nuances of the original languages helps us enter into the biblical text more personally, competently, and confidently.

I have learned far more about biblical interpretation, particularly with respect to my own personal and group exegetical experience, from Martini's spirituality books than I have from academic textbooks, which are often dry and overly technical. Likewise, Pope Benedict XVI has frequently pointed out the sterility of the historical-critical method (modern biblical criticism—criticim being an attempt to identify the subject's essential meaning), when divorced from the Bible's spiritual roots. Martini helps readers to relate the biblical text and drama in relation to their life experiences, and apply what they are learning.

Following in the Bible's and Church's footsteps, Martini balances prudential restraint and imagination in exercising creative but responsible freedom in interpreting and applying the Bible. He approaches and shares the Bible responsibly, respectfully, prudently, humbly, hopefully, and enthusiastically rather than defensively or polemically.

This world-class Scripture scholar is not obtuse or literalistic in his popular-level books and talks. He knowingly injects himself and his experience into the biblical texts, integrating the eisegetical (reading/projecting our perspective into the Bible in search of its personal or contemporary meaning) and exegetical (reading out of the Bible, or interpreting its literal meaning) dimensions. We should feel no inhibitions about attempting the same. Each of us brings a unique perspec-

Each of us brings a unique perspective, history, and potential to the Bible, so we should be confident and hopeful of encountering God and ourselves there in an authentic manner.

tive, history, and potential to the Bible, so we should be confident and hopeful of encountering God and ourselves there in an authentic manner.

Remember, we are seeking the message intended for us individually and communally, so there is no need to dwell on larger, abstract, technical issues. That is the domain of scholars and leaders in the Church, who are nonetheless called to experience the personal dimension as well. The doctrinal implications of the Bible have their place in our spirituality, but are negated if we do not experience and respond to God's personal invitation.

Authentic biblical interpretation and application is a lifelong struggle to integrate the literal, historical, exegetical meaning of the Bible with its personal, contemporary, eisegetical meaning. With the Holy Spirit's and Church's assistance, we can manage this tension in a healthy, efficacious, albeit imperfect manner, so that the historical and timeless meanings of the Bible come together in our heart and experience. We are invited to ponder, live and share the Bible in dialogue with God's ongoing initiative in our life (providence). Martini often speaks of the Bible's dynamism, the way its meaning and values continue to unfold within each person and generation.

The Personal Touch

In giving workshops and weekend retreats on *lectio divina*, I have experienced a similar phenomenon. I can't give retreatants enough process or practice time. The more I give, the more they want. The Bible is contagious. Adults in particular learn by doing.

When we practice interpreting and praying with the Bible, we make a marvelous discovery. Accompanied on our journey by the Spirit and fellow Christians, we can understand, apply, and implement God's message to us. This book is designed to support that process. I look forward to learning from you how well it has achieved that goal.

- As you become more comfortable with the Bible, and presuming that you use a reasonably literal translation that is consistent in its translation of key words (all translations recommended in this book meet this criteria), pay attention to grammar and vocabulary. The style, syntax, and vocabulary in which something is expressed offer clues to its meaning. The medium is part of the message.

- Pay attention to repetition. The inspired writers didn't have the option of underlining, highlighting, italicizing or using exclamation points, so they used repetition for emphasis. If something is repeated in the Bible, it is probably significant.

- Expect truth and integrity, rather than perfection and linear consistency, from the Bible. If the Bible was perfect in an absolute sense it wouldn't be fully human. It would be too much for us, and we'd be overwhelmed. Vatican II's classic and oft-quoted statement on inerrancy is fittingly nuanced:

"Those divinely revealed realities which are contained and presented in Sacred Scripture have been committed to writing under the inspiration of the Holy Spirit. For holy mother Church, relying on the belief of the Apostles (see John 20:31; 2 Tim. 3:16; 2 Peter 1:19-20, 3:15-16), holds that the books of both the Old and New Testaments in their entirety, with all their parts, are sacred and canonical because, written under the inspiration of the Holy Spirit, they have God as their author and have been handed on as such to the Church herself. In composing the sacred books, God chose men and while employed by Him they made use of their powers and abilities, so that with Him acting in them and through them, they, as true authors, consigned to writing everything and only those things which He wanted.

"Therefore, since everything asserted by the inspired authors or sacred writers must be held to be asserted by the Holy Spirit, it follows that the books of Scripture must be acknowledged as teaching solidly, faithfully and without error that truth which God wanted put into sacred writings for the sake of salvation. Therefore 'all Scripture is divinely inspired and has its use for teaching the truth and refuting error, for reformation of manners and discipline in right living, so that the man who belongs to God may be efficient and equipped for good work of every kind' " (2 Tim. 3:16-17, Greek text).

(*Dei Verbum,* Dogmatic Constitution of Divine Revelation, 11).

The Bible is a human as well as divine document, and like everything human it has rough edges. Just as we endeavor to balance Jesus' humanity and divinity in order to understand Him, so we must do the same with the Bible. When we over-emphasize either of its dimensions, we distort its message.

- Always bear in mind the primary purpose for which the Bible was written: to reconcile God and the world. Resist temptations to interpret the Bible in a way foreign to the objectives and circumstances of its original author(s) and audience—for example, according to modern scientific, cultural, or literary standards. Using the example of feminist hermeneutics (the science of interpretation), the Pontifical Biblical Commission's 1993 document *The Interpretation of the Bible in the Church* likewise warned of the dangers of imposing modern concepts and concerns on the biblical text such that we distort its literal meaning and confuse it with its contemporary or applied meaning.

While the Bible has a timeless dimension, it also is a product of its times. The more familiar we are with the Bible's human context, the less likely we will project our personal and cultural bias into the text in the name of exegesis (literal interpretation of the Bible).

Eisegesis, or projecting ourselves into the Bible, has its place in the interpretive process as long as we do not confuse it with exegesis. Humility, fraternal feedback and correction, and divine mercy enable us to mitigate and cope with the negative consequences of such confusion.

Keep in mind the parallel between Jesus' and the Bible's human nature. Both were subject to human limitations and conditions, but that doesn't mean that either is flawed or less than divine. Jesus and the Bible don't *transcend* limitations as much as they *transform* them into opportunities for conversion and growth (cf. 2 Cor 5:21).

- One of the great contributions of the modern papacy and Vatican II has been the way it has artfully, prudently, and respectfully assimilated the human sciences into its cosmology, anthropology, and pastoral theology. Properly integrated, neither spirituality nor science need be compromised. Judicious use of autonomous disciplines such as archaeology, phenomenology, history, literary criticism, sociology, and psychology can enhance interpretation and application of the Bible.

Awareness of the Church's discerning incorporation of the human sciences prepares you for biblical commentaries, footnotes, and background sources that utilize the insights of these modern disciplines.

- Writing in your Bible or journal is a good way to record insights and feelings evoked by the Bible. It helps you discern, interpret, and respond appropriately to significant events and circumstances in the Bible and life. It can help you identify parallels between events and circumstances in your life and the Bible. A wide-margin Bible, one with generous white space in the margins, makes this convenient.

See my book *Journaling with Moses and Job* for guidance on using *lectio divina* and biblical spirituality principles in conjunction with journaling.

- Affirm yourself and thank God when you read or apply the Bible despite fatigue, lethargy, discouragement or confusion. Make the necessary adjustments and corrections when you become negligent in reading or living the Bible, ask God for assistance and forgiveness, and move forward. God moves beyond our sins quicker than we do (cf. Ps 103:12; Is 43:25; Jer 31:34; Heb 10:17).

My weaknesses, wounds, and disappointments have been the context of my greatest insights into the Bible, life, and myself. Discerned experience purified by prayer, dialogue, and truth (of which Scripture is an inspired, accessible, and incomparable source) is the best teacher. In the Bible, God is continually reaching out to the downtrodden and commanding us to do the same.

- We should extend compassion, understanding, and outreach to ourselves as well. As observed by the Swiss psychiatrist Carl Jung in a popular essay, we too are "the least of these" (cf. Mt 25:31-46) and should respond accordingly. How often we forget or overlook this and neglect pastoral care to ourselves; consequently, we find ourselves drained and unable to extend such care to others.

This compassion is based not on our innate goodness, obscured and compromised by sin, but on God's limitless mercy, manifested for all times in the gift of His Son and Spirit.

- Bible reading is not meant to be a solitary activity only. "Iron sharpens iron, and one man sharpens another" (Prov 27:17). When feasible, participate in Bible-sharing groups or classes. Communal prayer, *lectio divina*, and service outreach engage Jesus' involvement (cf. Mt 18:20). The Bible is a community book in its origins and applications. According to the Bible, and as particularly recognized in Catholic and Orthodox theology, salvation is understood as a communal as well as an individual affair.

Summary

Solidarity is a fitting note on which to conclude our dialogue and return to our source, the Bible. The familial, filial, evangelical, and ecumenical opportunities for solidarity in the Lord are endless.

There is always more to say about the Bible, but since it speaks for itself quite well I'll step aside and join you in returning to the Word. The Holy Spirit is our spokesperson in prayer (cf. Rom 8:26-27) and Scripture (cf. 2 Tim 3:16-17), so we should concentrate on attuning and disciplining ourselves to listen and respond.

If amid living out this mystery you have any questions or comments, or if I can be of service in any way, please let me know. An email (karlaschultz@ juno.com), letter (3431 Gass Avenue, Pittsburgh, PA 15212-2239), or phone call: (412) 766-7545 would be fine. Check out my website, *karlaschultz.com*, for details and updates on contact information, published materials, and speaking and media dates.

Thank you for your attentiveness and perseverance. Peace and blessings to you on your path.

Bibliography

General Works on the Bible

Boadt, Lawrence. *Reading the Old Testament: An Introduction.* Mahwah, NJ: Paulist Press, 1985.

Brown, Raymond E. *Responses to 101 Questions on the Bible.* Mahwah, NJ: Paulist Press, 1990.

——. *An Introduction to the New Testament.* New York: Doubleday, 1997. (Reference work for intermediate and advanced readers.)

Brown, Raymond E., Fitzmyer, Joseph A., and Murphy, Roland E. (editors). *The New Jerome Biblical Commentary.* New York: Prentice Hall, Inc., 1990. The best one-volume Catholic commentary. The original JBC, though dated (1968), remains useful.

Charpentier, Etienne. *How to Read the Bible.* New York: Gramercy Books, 1991.

Kodell, Jerome. *The Catholic Bible Study Handbook: A Popular Introduction to Studying Scripture.* Ann Arbor, MI: Servant Books, 2001.

Martin, George. *Reading Scripture as the Word of God.* Ann Arbor, MI: Servant Books, 1998. (This is its fourth edition. That says something about its popularity and durability.)

——. *Bringing the Gospel of Matthew to Life.* Ijamsville, MD: The Word Among Us Press, 2008.

——. *Praying with Jesus: What the Gospels Tell Us About How to Pray.* Chicago, IL: Loyola Press, 2000.

Martini, Cardinal Carlo. *The Gospel According to St. Paul.* Tr. Marsha Daigle-Williamson. Ijamsville, MD: The Word Among Us Press, 2008.

Montague, George, T. *Understanding the Bible: A Basic Introduction to Biblical Interpretation.* Mahwah, NJ: Paulist Press, 1997.

Murphy, Richard, T.A. *Background to the Bible.* Ann Arbor, MI: Servant Books, 1978.

Ska, Jean-Louis. *Introduction to Reading the Pentateuch.* Winona Lake, IN: Eisenbrauns, 2006.

Wijngaards, John. *Handbook to the Gospels.* Ann Arbor, MI: Servant Books, 1979.

Winkler, Jude. *The Gospels: Simply Explained.* Totowa, NJ: Catholic Book Publishing Corp., 2008.

Lectio Divina

Christian Prayer, the official one-volume edition of the *Liturgy of the Hours*, with complete texts of Morning and Evening Prayer for the entire year. (Totowa, NJ: Catholic Book Publishing Corp., 1976).

Liturgy of the Hours, the official four-volume English edition of the Divine Office that contains the translation of the International Committee on English in the Liturgy approved by the Episcopal Conference of the U.S. and 26 other English-speaking countries. (Totowa, NJ: Catholic Book Publishing Corp., 1975/1976).

Shorter Christian Prayer, with Morning and Evening Prayer from the Four-Week Psalter and selected texts for the Seasons and Major Feasts of the year. A user-friendly, portable version of the above. (Totowa, NJ: Catholic Book Publishing Corp., 1988).

Binz, Stephen J. *Conversing with God in Scripture: A Contemporary Approach to Lectio Divina.* Ijamsville, MD: The Word Among Us Press, 2008.

Brook, John. *The School of Prayer: An Introduction to the Divine Office for All Christians.* Collegeville, MN: The Liturgical Press, 1992.

Casey, Michael. *Sacred Reading: The Ancient Art of Lectio Divina.* Liguori, MO: Liguori/Triumph, 1995.

Deiss, Lucien. *Celebration of the Word.* Collegeville, MN: The Liturgical Press, 1993.

Guigo II. *The Ladder of Monks and Twelve Meditations.* Translated by Edmund Colledge and James Walsh. Kalamazoo, MI: Cistercian Publications, 1981. (Classic medieval work on *lectio divina.*)

Hall, Thelma. *Too Deep for Words: Rediscovering Lectio Divina.* Mahwah, NJ: Paulist Press, 1988.

Johnson, Maxwell E. *Benedictine Daily Prayer: A Short Breviary.* Collegeville, MN: The Liturgical Press, 2005.

Leclercq, Dom Jean. *The Love of Learning and the Desire for God.* New York: Mentor Omega Books, 1962. (Classic modern work on *lectio divina.*)

Magrassi, Mariano. *Praying the Bible: An Introduction to Lectio Divina.* Collegeville, MN: The Liturgical Press, 1998.

Masini, Mario. *Lectio Divina: An Ancient Prayer That Is Ever New.* Staten Island, NY: Alba House, 1998.

Miller, Charles E. *Together in Prayer: Learning to Love the Liturgy of the Hours.* Staten Island, NY: Alba House, 1994.

Nugent, Madeline. *The Divine Office for Dodos.* Totowa, NJ: Catholic Book Publishing Corp., 2008.

Pennington, M. Basil. *Lectio Divina: Renewing the Ancient Practice of Praying the Scriptures.* New York: The Crossroad Publishing Company, 1998.

Sullivan, Shirley. *A Companion to the Liturgy of the Hours: Morning and Evening Prayer* (Totowa, NJ: Catholic Book Publishing Corp., 2004).

Toon, Peter. *The Art of Meditating on Scripture.* Grand Rapids, MI: Zondervan, 1993.

Works by the Author

Schultz, Karl A. *Where Is God When You Need Him?: Sharing Stories of Suffering with Job and Jesus.* Staten Island, NY: Alba House, 1992.

——. *The Art and Vocation of Caring for Persons in Pain.* Mahwah, NJ: Paulist Press, 1994.

——. *Personal Energy Management: A Christian Personal and Professional Development Program.* Chicago: Loyola University Press, 1994.

——. *Nourished by the Word: A Dialogue with Brother Andrew Campbell, O.S.B. on Praying the Scriptures and Holistic Personal Growth.* Notre Dame, IN: Ave Maria Press, 1994.

——. *Journaling with Moses and Job.* Boston: Pauline Books & Media, 1996.

——. *Job Therapy.* Pittsburgh, PA: Genesis Personal Development Center, 1996.

——. *Personal Energy Manager Rainbow Planner.* Pittsburgh, PA: Genesis Personal Development Center, 1997.

——. *Calming the Stormy Seas of Stress.* Winona, MN: St. Mary's Press, 1998.

——. *The How-To Book of the Bible.* Huntington, IN: Our Sunday Visitor, 2004.

Schultz, Karl A. and Lorene Hanley Duquin. *The Bible and You.* Huntington, IN: Our Sunday Visitor, 2005.

Schultz, Karl A. *Becoming Community.* New York: New City Press, 2007.

——. *Pope Paul VI: Christian Virtues and Values.* New York: Crossroad Publishing Company, 2007.

——. *Bearing the Unbearable: Coping with Infertility and Other Profound Suffering.* Ann Arbor, MI: Nimble Books, 2007.

——. *How to Pray with the Bible: The Ancient Prayer Form of Lectio Divina Made Simple.* Huntington, IN: Our Sunday Visitor, 2007.

The above books, along with audiotapes, CDs, and DVDs of the author's presentations on *lectio divina* and other biblical spirituality and personal growth subjects can be ordered from Genesis Personal Development Center, 3431 Gass Avenue, Pittsburgh, PA, 15212-2239. The e-mail address is karlaschultz@juno.com, and the web site is *karlaschultz.com*. The phone number is (412) 766-7545.

About the Author

Karl A. Schultz is the director of Genesis Personal Development Center in Pittsburgh. He is one of the world's most prolific authors and speakers on *lectio divina,* the Church's oldest and official model for prayerfully reading Scripture. He has published twelve books and one audiocassette and has presented programs on *lectio divina,* biblical spirituality, men's spirituality, gender relations and communications, time and stress management, organizational development, caregiving, and suffering in corporate, healthcare, church, state, association, convention, and retreat environments throughout the United States. He has been interviewed on several EWTN programs, including *Bookmark, Living His Life Abundantly, Life on the Rock,* and *EWTN Live!*

St. Joseph Bibles and Missals

No. 612/97—Family Bible—White Padded Leather

No. 609/13—Deluxe Leather Bible—Brown, White or Red

No. 825/23—Daily and Sunday Missal—3-Volume Set

Liturgy of the Hours

No. 409/10—Set of 4 volumes—Flexible Binding

No. 409/13—Set of 4 volumes—Leather Binding

No. 709/13—Set of 4 volumes—Large-print, Leather binding

No. 406/10—*Christian Prayer*—Flexible maroon binding

No. 406/23—*Christian Prayer*—Zipper binding

No. 408/10—*Shorter Christian Prayer*—Flexible binding

No. 415/04—*A Companion to the Liturgy of the Hours: Morning and Evening Prayer*

No. 416/04—*The Divine Office for Dodos: A Step-by-Step Guide to Praying the Liturgy of the Hours*—By Madeline Pecora Nugent

No. 426/04—*Practical Guide to the Liturgy of the Hours*—By Shirley Sullivan

For free catalog contact
www.catholicbookpublishing.com